SMART IDEAS
FOR TOP-NOTCH COLLECTING

Your stamp collection can bring you hours of fun and years of pleasure. The aim of ~~this~~ ~~book~~ ~~to~~ ~~help~~ ~~you~~ ~~get~~ ~~the~~ ~~most~~ is to insure that your p~~leasure~~ ~~is~~ ~~endless~~ ~~and~~ ~~to~~~~tally satisfying, and deep~~~~ly~~ ~~rewarding~~ ~~no~~ ~~matter~~ ~~your~~ age or income level.

No other guide gives you ~~the~~ ~~kind~~ ~~of~~ ~~valuable~~ ~~in~~~~formation about creating~~ ~~and~~ ~~maintaining~~ ~~a~~ ~~superb~~, ~~im~~~~pressive collection. Some of the important facts you'll dis~~cover in this essential volume are:

- THE BEST WAYS TO PROTECT YOUR STAMPS

- EXPERT ADVICE ON SPOTTING THE BEST STAMP BARGAINS

- THE ABC'S OF USING STAMP CATALOGS—THE PHILATELIST'S "BIBLES"

- INSIDERS' TIPS ON STAMPS FROM THE WORLD'S MOST INTRIGUING SMALL COUNTRIES

- PRICING VARIATIONS ON STAMPS OVER THE YEARS

- HOW TO FOLLOW TRENDS AND SPOT THE "HOTTEST" COUNTRIES TO COLLECT

THOROUGHLY UP-TO-DATE AND RELIABLE

CHARLES ADAMS'S
STAMP COLLECTING

STAMP COLLECTING

THE COMPLETE EASY GUIDE TO THE WORLD'S MOST POPULAR HOBBY

—

Charles F. Adams

A DELL BOOK

Published by
Dell Publishing
a division of
Bantam Doubleday Dell Publishing Group, Inc.
666 Fifth Avenue
New York, New York 10103

ISBN: 0-440-21007-0

Printed in the United States of America

Published simultaneously in Canada

May 1992

10 9 8 7 6 5 4 3 2 1

OPM

CONTENTS

Contents

ACKNOWLEDGMENTS

For a project that seemed so simple in its concept, the creation of this little book has required the participation and help of an awful lot of people. I am grateful to all of them, and especially to the following:

At Dell, special thanks to Leslie Schnur whose idea this book was in the first place, and to Jeanne Cavelos, my editor, who has asked me the right questions, given me lots of support, and *been very patient*.

Thanks to Susan and Paul Gilbert for loan of their country house so I could concentrate for a few days. Major thanks to Connie Salavarria who provided the line drawings for the book, and to Stan Newman who took all the pictures—both now know more about stamps than they ever thought they would.

Thanks as well to my mother, Ruby Adams, who allowed me as a child to make such a mess with my stamps. And greatest thanks of all to Bob Donaghey, philatelic partner *par excellence,* who typed, critiqued, cajoled, and even added a few words here and there—quite literally, I couldn't have done it without him.

PREFACE

It all started innocently enough. An aunt, herself a collector of any and everything—a kind of rural bag lady—must have recognized a kindred spirit in me. When I was very young she gave me an envelope filled with stamps, with corners torn from envelopes, some of them many years old. Most were familiar designs with pictures of George Washington or of Franklin or Lincoln; a few were more exotic—stamps from England and France and Germany.

"What am I going to do with these?" I asked myself.

"Become a stamp collector," a little voice replied.

"Oh, okay," I responded, and never looked back.

Actually it was a kind of revelation. Here were these little pieces of paper. I'd been seeing them for years—nine to be exact—but now they took on a whole new meaning. Yes, I would collect them.

And so it began.

I put the stamps in a notebook, neatly arranged in rows. When that notebook was filled, I started another. And then another. For hours I sat in my room, soaking these stamps from their envelopes, drying them, then patiently arranging them on pages. This was great. I could do this forever.

My aunt, great source of raw material that she was, soon ran out of old envelopes. What now? I wondered. Obviously I had to have more stamps, so I would just have to search elsewhere. My mother, a woman blessed with a more practical and therefore not especially sentimental outlook on life, was not a hoarder like my aunt. In fact, she had not saved much of anything. Well, maybe last year's Christmas cards, so she would know who should be on her list for this year, but none of those neat things my aunt had given me. No, my mother wasn't going to be any help.

Then another aunt, not a farmer's wife but married to a soldier, went to live in Germany. I practically swooned when my Christmas present that year included a box full of stamps she had collected for me. But Christmas didn't happen often enough. What would I do for the other months?

Salvation came on a matchbook. Back when it was still okay to smoke, you could find ads for stamp collectors on matchbook covers. They were those "100 stamps—worldwide—all different—for 10 cents" kinds of ads. Well, I answered all of them. Soon stamps were pouring in—stamps from everywhere, even places I'd never heard of. I was in heaven.

More stamps meant more notebooks, more arranging. Unfortunately, there was that ten cents to be reckoned with (multiplied many times over), and that meant finding ways to increase my allowance. This need became especially intense when I discovered that there were actual stamp albums, divided into countries, and with pictures of the stamps, showing me where to put them and everything.

This was great. This was incredible! Soon I was a child obsessed. I had to fill those pages!

In many ways, I guess, I am still a child obsessed. I have enjoyed a lifelong love affair with stamps and stamp collecting—that part of the child has never left me. The sense of discovery that comes with stamps, the constant learning and relearning, that absurd passion to accumulate —these have never left me either. Some things have changed, of course. The notebooks have been replaced by sophisticated albums, and now it is not enough just to treasure my collection, I have to insure it as well. But the joy is still there, and I don't think it will ever go away.

It is my goal to share some of this passion with you. And hopefully I will be able to give you some seasoned advice on how to go about collecting stamps for yourself. There is so much to learn, so much fun to be had. Enjoy.

What Constitutes
a Stamp Collection

—

Why are you doing this? What on earth has possessed you, or more likely, what unearthly force has driven you to be gathering these scraps of paper—used paper, at that!—and sticking them in books?

You don't know . . . right?

And chances are, you don't care either. Because the simple truth is, some of us are born male, some female; some with brown eyes, some with blue; some left-handed, some right; some to be stamp collectors, and some not. You see, it's not really a choice you make—it's fate, and there's nothing you can do about it.

Well, if you're one of these stamps collectors to nature-born, you can take comfort in the knowledge that you are not alone. In fact, stamp collecting, or philately, as it is properly known, is the most popular hobby in the world. In the United States alone there are millions of individual collectors. Additionally there are hundreds of stamp clubs across the country, ranging from highly sophisticated organizations boasting world class collections to elementary school groups who meet primarily to share and swap their finds.

And as I've said already, the one thing that all philatelists have in common is passion, a love of the hobby, a desire to spend countless hours searching, sorting, cataloguing, collecting these little pieces of paper. Indeed, putting together a stamp collection is a fairly major commitment timewise, and it can, if you allow it, become a substantial financial investment as well. It needn't be expensive, however, for there are all sorts of ways one can go about collecting, and there are many different types of collections.

The one thing a collector must accept from the outset —unless, perhaps, your name is Rockefeller or Trump, or you run a middle eastern nation, or you've won the Florida lottery, or you're a sports hero—is that you will never, never, ever, ever fill every space in every stamp album. There are just too many countries who've issued too many stamps, and some of these stamps are distressingly rare and therefore *expensive*.

Actually, it may surprise some of you who are just beginning to collect that there are whole companies—large companies—that exist solely to meet the needs (and, let's face it, *create* the needs) of the millions of collectors worldwide. Of course, they provide a great service to collectors, but when you're just starting out and you figure you might as well begin with the deluxe edition of everything, it is pretty disheartening to find out, hey! this stuff is not cheap! No, but the fact is, it doesn't *have* to be expensive.

So back to my initial point: forget about collecting each and every stamp ever issued by each and every country. Of course, if you're so possessed—and more than a little demented, as I am—you can prepare yourself for that goal by

Cats are not necessarily the best stamp collecting companions, but they seem to like the hobby, so why not?

having albums that have spaces for every stamp ever issued. But as for filling them—well, you'll have a lot of fun anyway.

So what is a stamp collection?

It's whatever you want it to be. Not everyone feels compelled to pursue the impossible, and not everyone has to spend a lot of money to enjoy his or her collection. It doesn't matter that you may never have an accumulation of stamps so unique that they merit public exhibition. It doesn't matter that you may never have a collection worth thousands of dollars. What *does* matter is that you enjoy what you're doing, that you get great satisfaction from it. In the process you will derive all sorts of ancillary benefits from it, and you will learn a lot about this world and its countries, its governments, and, especially, its people. Philately is a hobby that can give you a solid grounding in geography and political and cultural history, while providing at the same time hours of discovery and fun.

So again I ask, "What is a stamp collection?"

POSTAGE STAMPS

Well, let's start with the world, all the countries that we hear about on the news and read about in newspapers, books, magazines. Each and every one of these countries issues stamps for use as postage. In the scheme of things, stamps are a relatively recent development. The first stamp issued by a national government appeared in 1840, a one-penny denomination put out by Great Britain. In only a few years, virtually all governments had followed suit, with the United States issuing its first stamps in 1847.

Some countries, especially smaller ones like the Scandinavian nations—Sweden, Denmark, Norway, Iceland, Finland—for many years issued a relatively small number of stamps. Others, like Mexico, Russia, and France, produced a fairly great variety of issues almost from the outset. Today, virtually every country issues a huge variety of postage material, much of it obviously geared to the collector first, its use for paying postage a far second in consideration. Some countries—San Marino, Paraguay, Hungary, and the various Arab Emirates, for example—seem to have made a major industry of issuing stamps solely for collectors; at times it gets a little overwhelming.

Overwhelming or not, however, chances are that once you begin to collect, you will soon have stamps from just about every nation. So for a while at least, just take stamps from wherever they come. You may eventually decide to go ahead and deal with all of them, contenting yourself with organizing these stamps from all parts of the world, accepting the fact that no one country may ever be nearly complete, but enjoying the variety you amass.

Chances are you will eventually develop a few favorites

—countries which for various reasons may seem most desirable to collect. Obviously the stamps of your own country are the most easily accessible and therefore the most convenient to begin collecting. The United States Postal Service has a particularly active program geared to encourage and assist stamp collectors. Most other countries have the same services, however, and are more than delighted to assist the foreign collector. Rest assured, if you want to collect stamps, there are seemingly endless numbers of organizations anxious to assist you. Few things come free, however, and in the next chapter we will deal in some detail with these various sources of stamps.

Okay, so let's say you have been gathering stamps for some time. It seems obvious that the United States is one country you might collect—there is a great variety of stamps, they can be found used all over the place, and mint copies of any current and many recent issues can be bought for face value at just about any post office. Even many older issues are quite inexpensive and are readily available from numerous stamp dealers. It will become more difficult, however, when you later start to fill in gaps in your collection, since some stamps are relatively scarce and trade at substantial cost. But don't worry. It will take you quite a while to reach that point in your collection. The United States has issued several thousand stamps, and most of these are easy and inexpensive to come by.

What about other countries? Canada is a good country to consider. Today it issues some of the most interesting stamps of any nation, and its proximity to the United States means that for many years its stamps have been crossing the border with regularity. Ditto, Mexico, although the postal service there has issued an incredible number of stamps over the past few years, and their characteristic seems to have been quantity over quality.

Also, just look at your collection. Is there a country, or maybe two or three, from which you have a substantial

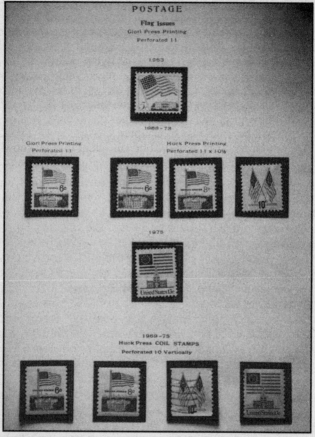

A page from the Scott U.S. Album displaying a variety of flag issues.

number of stamps? If so, then you should consider starting with these.

Or maybe there is one country that so intrigues you that you want to collect its stamps, whether or not there are any in your collection at present. Before you set your heart on it, check out the prices for some of that country's stamps—there may be a good reason why there are none in your collection. (As to how to determine the value of stamps of any given country, the rather complex system of valuation will be discussed in Chapter 4. Skip ahead if you like, although for now it should be sufficient just to know there is a simple way of determining a value for virtually every stamp ever issued.)

One of the great joys and benefits of stamp collecting is the rather remarkable history lesson one learns more or less by osmosis. And of course you're bound to absorb a fair share of global geography as well. Part of this knowledge could be put to use deciding what countries to emphasize in your collection. For example, Israel came into existence as a nation in 1948; the government promptly began to issue stamps and has done so relentlessly ever since. The point is, however, Israel didn't even exist for the full first one hundred years of philatelic history, and most of its many (many, many) stamps are relatively easy to collect. They also happen to be especially beautiful, since they were geared for collectors almost from the outset.

Then there are other countries which not only have a relatively recent beginning, they also have an even more recent end. When World War I ended, a lot of eastern Europe got chopped up, renamed, and redistributed. Estonia, Latvia, and Lithuania were three such countries. Formed in 1918, immediately after World War I, they existed as independent nations—issuing postage stamps, of course—until World War II, when they disappeared behind the Iron Curtain, becoming a part of the U.S.S.R., their individual stamps replaced by those of Russia. Today, with the new independence of these countries, you can expect to see the issuance of new stamps bearing a national designation. When they were previously independent, these countries—particularly Latvia—issued stamps of singularly arresting design, and many of them are surprisingly easy and affordable to collect. As you become more familiar with the stamps in your collection as well as the diverse realm of stamps available to collectors, you will no doubt determine your own individual favorite countries to collect.

It seems appropriate to include here a few words about an ongoing controversy in philatelic circles. I have already alluded to countries that seem to exist solely to print stamps for the collector. In fact, there are some "countries" that do issue stamps only for the purpose of deriving income from sale to collectors, and it becomes a major project to search for stamps from these countries which have actually been postally used. Many appear to be used because they have been canceled to order (or CTO, as it is commonly known in philatelic jargon), and most likely have been printed—and canceled—by a licensing outfit which blithely prints and cancels these stamps and then sells them exclusively to dealers. For example, the tiny middle eastern Kingdom of Umm al Qaiwain has issued hundreds of different stamps—many of them very attractive— all of them printed and distributed from points in western Europe or the United States.

So are these really stamps, then? They look like stamps, but they were never actually meant for postal use. Thus, purists—and others of us not so pure—are disdainful of these ersatz stamps and do not include them in our collections. Does this mean you should also ignore these stamps? It is totally up to you, and the answer lies in what you want to get out of collecting. If you want to establish a first-rate, competition-class collection, worth many thousands of dollars, then these stamps have no place in your collection. On the other hand, if you just want to have fun, and are collecting for the sheer joy of it, then why not? Remember there are no rules in this hobby, at least when it

An example of a sheet of stamps precanceled, technically "used" but never actually used as postage. The gum on the back is still intact.

comes to what you collect. Your collection is yours to develop as you see fit, and in the end its makeup will be determined by and will be a reflection of your interests and your personality.

United Nations Postal Administration

As a worldwide governing body and an administrative office with its own territory (a few acres in New York City), the United Nations issues its own stamps for use on mail originating at its headquarters building.

The first United Nations stamps were issued in October of 1957, some ten years after the organization was created. Once it began to issue stamps, however, it proceeded with gusto, and in the intervening years has created hundreds of different issues.

U.N. stamps are generally quite beautiful and therefore are especially attractive to collectors. These stamps are additionally attractive because they carry a message of international peace, and a portion of the money raised through their sale goes to help support various U.N. help-giving organizations.

Because the U.N. is aware that most of its stamps are sold to collectors, special efforts are made to cater to their needs and requirements. In addition to issuing stamps of unique beauty that contain images of international appeal and interest, the U.N. post office takes special care in the cancellation of postally used stamps. The postal agency issues regular bulletins announcing new philatelic issues, and offers a subscription procedure to collectors whereby you can place a standing order for new stamps and they are sent to you automatically.

TOPICALS

Which brings us to another area of collecting. Let's say you've amassed a quantity of stamps, but when you look at them you are less drawn to national characteristics or designations than you are to the subject matter of individual stamps. For example, you might find that you have a number of stamps that have ships on them, so you might decide to concentrate on collecting stamps that either have depictions of actual ships on them, or are in some other way nautical, no matter what countries they may come from. Such grouping would constitute a *topical* collection.

Topicals represent a major area of philately and effectively serve to allow the collector to customize his or her collection to suit individual tastes.

There are seemingly endless areas for topical designation, although some are obviously more popular and common than others. Ships was one area mentioned; others may include cats, flowers, reptiles, maps, horses, presidents, works of art, birds, dancers, and on and on. Some areas are more likely to yield a greater selection of stamps than others. Flowers, for example, have been regularly depicted on stamps of all nations for many years, and new ones are always being issued. Some topicals are so popular that albums are available with places for virtually all stamps issued in that special area. Walt Disney characters —yes, Walt Disney characters—have been granted just such an album, and there are hundreds of collectors who enjoy this particular pursuit. For what it's worth, most "Mickey Mouse" stamps have been issued by those countries we discussed earlier who put out seemingly thousands of stamps intended only for use by collectors—the Caribbean nations in particular seem to be fond of Mickey and his friends. In fact, these are colorful, clever, and generally well-executed stamps, and they *are* fun to collect.

One of the great advantages of a topical collection is that it allows you to explore the stamps of every nation, crossing borders at will. It also allows you to organize your collection in any way you see fit, customizing it to your own satisfaction. Topicals also are a relatively inexpensive way to get started in collecting, especially if one chooses a popular area of interest. Take ships, for example: there are

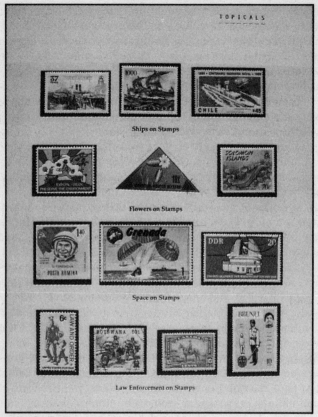

A page of popular topicals from various countries.

hundreds of stamps from every nation that depict ships of some kind, and most of these can be had very cheaply.

Or you may choose to collect stamps in a very narrow or special area. Say, movie stars are your thing—there aren't thousands of stamps for you to choose from, but there are enough of them available for you to have fun.

Or let's say you are really into specialization, maybe stamps featuring Winston Churchill—again, there are many more available than you might suspect.

The point is, if you decide to pursue one or more topical areas for collection, there are a great variety of stamps available from all countries. It is a tremendously satisfying and educational way of collecting stamps and is increasingly popular.

SPECIALIZED AND BACK-OF-THE-BOOK COLLECTIONS

There are many ways to customize a collection. Some collectors—generally the most serious philatelists, those who love the hobby so much they turn it into a virtual second career—specialize to a point that the casual or novice philatelist may find difficult to comprehend. These people generally have studied an area of postal history so thoroughly that they become experts in that area, and thus they focus their collections to reflect this overwhelming interest.

Obviously this is no way to begin as a collector, but it is something to keep in mind as you learn about the overlap of postal history with other historical developments. During World War II, for example, a great deal of mail crossing national borders was opened by government censors who read the contents to make sure no secrets were being passed to the enemy. The envelopes in these cases were dutifully marked by the censors, sometimes routinely, at other times with special notations. The result today is a very popular area of specialized collecting.

There is no limit to the ways you can narrow or focus your collection, if you choose. As you learn more about stamps and about postal history, you may well find an area which is of particular interest to you.

Or you may decide on a more arbitrary way of special-

Topicals

The collection of topical stamps—from all nations, but each with a common theme—is an especially popular area of philately. There is virtually no limit to the kinds of topics one may choose to collect, although some offer greater opportunity than others. The following is a list of some of the more popular subjects:

Airplanes
Automobiles
Birds
Boy Scouts
Butterflies
Cats
Christopher Columbus
Costumes and clothing
Disney characters
Dogs
Fish
Flags of nations
Flowers
Horses
Music
Olympics
Paintings of the masters
Presidents of the United States
Red Cross
Religion
Royal weddings
Ships
Space
Sports
Transportation
World War II
Zeppelins

ization, for example, collecting all the stamps issued by all nations the year you were born. Certainly when you look at such a collection you get a strong sense of what was going on that year politically and culturally.

Another way of specializing is to focus on stamps which are part of what is generally called the "back-of-the-book." The term will be more comprehensible when you learn all about traditional stamp albums and catalogues in later chapters. It's sufficient at this point to know that stamps so called were regularly issued items, but were meant for some special postal usage. For example, airmail stamps are back-of-the-book items, as are special delivery, official, and any number of other categories. Typically many fewer of these stamps have been issued than of regular postage stamps.

One area of special interest to collectors is that of semipostal or "charity" stamps. You won't find any of these in your U.S. collection, however, for this country's government has generally seen fit to leave collecting monies for charity use to the private sector. Quite simply, these stamps are used as postage, but cost more than the regular stamp; so, if the cost of mailing a letter were twenty-five cents (ah, remember the days!), one might buy a stamp marked twenty-five cents + five cents, the extra nickel going to charity. Many countries—especially France, Germany, Belgium, the Netherlands, and Switzerland—have traditionally issued numerous semipostal stamps, often of especially attractive design. Any of the back-of-the-book areas can be rewarding and fun to collect; again, it is simply a matter of your own personal interests.

Be Your Own Postmaster

The U.S. Postal Service is essentially a monopoly—they don't like competition, they won't tolerate it, and there are laws to protect their status as sole carrier of the mails.

These laws don't prevent you from creating your own personalized stamps, however, and you can get an official permit that authorizes you to create a hand stamp to use in canceling even U.S. stamps.

As for your own stamps, they must be used in conjunction with valid U.S. stamps or your mail won't move beyond the mail box, but they do provide you the opportunity of making a personal statement with every letter you mail.

Likewise, you can ensure that your own town's name appears as part of the cancellation if you create your own hand stamp. Use of such a hand stamp requires a permit, but it is available for free. To get a permit, pick up an application available at any post office; ask for form No. 3620. The post office will assign you a number that must be used on the hand stamp, and there are standards you must follow that regulate its size and design.

COVERS

Another increasingly popular area for collectors is that of covers, by which is meant quite simply the entire envelope with the stamp in place.

First day covers are envelopes mailed on the first day of issuance of a particular stamp. Typically the cancellation includes the date and location of the issuing post office, along with the designation "First Day of Issue." (Usually for the first day of issue, only one post office is designated as the point of origin; if, for example, the stamp depicts the Alamo, the chances are the first day's issue would be mailed exclusively from San Antonio, Texas.) Special, fancy envelopes, called "cachets," may also be used, some of which are quite elaborate. These cachets add nothing to the legitimacy of the cover, but they can be quite interesting and are usually more desirable to collectors.

Another kind of "cover" is simply any envelope with some distinguishing characteristic. For example, when airmail service was just beginning, envelopes carried on a particular route on the first day of service were often so designated, making them collectible. Other covers may be of interest because of the stamps used—say all ten designs from one issue on the same envelope—or perhaps because of the person to whom it is addressed.

The bottom line with covers is that if the particular envelope is of interest to you, then add it to your collection. You may value something even though no monetary or catalogue value is assigned to it. And some stamps are actually *more valuable* if they are left on the original envelope.

Some people want to collect only covers, preferring to display their stamps as they were actually used. One advantage to this method is that you don't have to worry about removing the stamp from the paper, and can thereby avoid the sometimes arduous task of soaking. A significant drawback, however, is that stamps are small and are easy to store and/or display, while stamps still on envelopes are quite another matter.

CINDERELLAS

Before getting to the ways of displaying your collection, however, there are still a few more kinds of collections to consider. One very popular area is what is commonly called "Cinderellas." These are items that look like stamps, but which were never meant for postal use. A very common example is the Christmas seal, issued annually in the United States since 1907. The practice began in Denmark, Sweden, and Iceland in 1904 for the purpose of raising money for charity. Many people collect Christmas seals, so many, in fact, that there is a catalogue price set for each U.S. issue.

Other charity "stamps"—Easter seals, for example—are also collected, along with any number of other unusual items which were typically issued for propaganda purposes, usually to be used in conjunction with postage on an envelope, but which themselves carried no monetary value. And, we can't forget Mormon stamps of Utah and the widely distributed Boys Town Stamps and stamps from Greenpeace and from all the various save-the-forest organizations that fill our mailboxes every day. Better than bills, I know, but still . . .

Not all "Cinderellas" come in the mail, of course. Other varieties include registration labels, telegraph stamps, transport company labels, private local stamps, rationing stamps, and on and on.

Once again, the only limiting factor in collecting "Cinderellas" is your own individual range of interest. If you want to collect them, then by all means do. "Cinderellas" are generally plentiful, usually free, often attractive, and an interesting adjunct to the standard postage stamp collection.

Complete covers can be of particular interest when Cinderellas have been mixed with standard postage. Look carefully, because sometimes—usually before computer automation was instituted—these "fake" stamps managed to pass as the real thing, and you may find a case where a Christmas seal, for example, may have been substituted for actual postage and has gotten through undetected.

REVENUES

One final major area of philatelic interest deserves discussion. Revenue stamps—or "revenues," as they are commonly called—have been issued much longer than have postage stamps. Simply put, revenue stamps are a tax, in the form of a piece of paper with a designated value that is attached to something else. So when you buy such a taxed item, you pay for the piece of paper as well—the extra money going to the government.

Revenues are much less common today than they used to be. Packs of playing cards, packs of cigarettes, bottles of wine, and bottles of many medicines are just a few examples of items that used to carry these stamps. (We still pay the added-value taxes, of course, it's just the stamps that have disappeared.) And remember those odd stamps that used to be found on tags attached to pillows, the kind that warned you "under penalty of law" not to remove them? Obviously many people failed to heed the warning, because these stamps, too, are fairly common in collections.

The most common revenue stamps, however, are those used in conjunction with legal documents. Transfer of property, for example, used to always entail the attachment of revenue stamps to the deed, presumably the government's way of covering its costs for keeping public records. These stamps are generally easier to collect than those mentioned earlier—let's face it, it's a lot simpler to get a stamp off an old deed than off an old medicine bottle— and also deeds are more likely to have been preserved.

You will also find that the federal government has had no monopoly on issuing added-value stamps. Some states have put their own tax on many items—those pillows, for example—and these stamps are revenues as well, although some purists might prefer to include these items among the Cinderellas.

Some people specialize in collecting revenues, to the exclusion of other philatelic items. Many collectors, however, consider them an attractive adjunct to their principal national collections. This is particularly true with collections focusing on Great Britain and countries that are or were part of the British Empire. Almost from the outset, these countries issued stamps that could be used either for postage or for paying revenue fees. As a result, one has to look carefully at the actual cancellation to see if a stamp

The collecting of "Cinderellas" and revenue stamps offers a lot in the way of variety.

has been used postally or fiscally. If you are a purist, you will not want any fiscally canceled (i.e., used to pay taxes) stamps mixed in with those used for postage. Those used for revenue purposes are generally of lesser value according to the accepted catalogue valuation.

Countries other than the United States and Great Britain and its colonies have also issued revenues, some of them of remarkable and/or exceptionally attractive design. Some of these stamps are a lot of fun to collect, although they have the disadvantage of being generally less readily available.

We have discussed several different forms your stamp collection may take, from the totally traditional to one customized to reflect your own personality. The point to remember as you go about putting your collection together—

which the rest of this book is aimed at assisting—is that you are doing this *because you want to,* and there are no boundaries, no rules for what you may include. There is a world of stamps out there; this is your collection. Have fun.

What you will encounter in the following chapters are groupings of information I think you will find them helpful as you set out to create your own individual stamp collection. I have attempted to include for discussion all those subjects and technical aspects of the hobby that I have found it necessary to understand. Some of them may seem confusing, even after you have read about them; over time, however, I think you will comprehend the distinctions.

Chapters 2 and 3 offer guidance in actually getting the stamps for your collection and in finding the best way for you to safely and practically house and display them.

Chapters 4 and 5 are essentially glossaries of terms that you will encounter as a collector. The first chapter deals with the more general terms of the hobby, while the second covers the terminology used to describe particular stamps or groups of stamps.

Chapter 6 consists of nuts-and-bolts descriptions of the various tools and philatelic devices available to collectors. An effort will be made to distinguish between those you need and those you need only if you become truly obsessive about the hobby.

Chapter 7 is a basic, rudimentary history of philately, and Chapter 8 is a more-or-less personal history of learning through stamps.

In the last chapter, Chapter 9, we delve into the very thorny area of stamp collecting as a form of investment, and I will announce right now that if you are reading this book because you are looking to make money with stamps, then skip to that chapter and save yourself the time it would take to read all that's in between.

Keep your focus all the while on just how wonderful stamp collecting is as a hobby, and you will learn a lot and won't be disappointed.

2

Putting Together a Collection: Where and How to Find Stamps

THE "COLLECTING" PART OF STAMP COLLECTING

Okay. So now you have a bunch of stamps. It's not too important where they came from. There are, however, two things that are important: Where do you get more? And what do you do and how do you treat them in order to protect them from damage?

When it comes to collecting stamps—and here I am speaking of the simple amassing of them—you should keep one thing in mind: each stamp is a potential mystery, and you should handle each and every one with care. Later you will understand more clearly what I mean by "mystery"; for now just trust me. Many times, things are not what they seem.

STALKING THE UPSIDE-DOWN JENNY

Something has gotten you started on this hobby, so presumably some dotty aunt or some such well-intentioned person has given you a cache of stamps. If you're really lucky, it's someone's old collection, already neatly mounted in a fat, shabby album. If you have been so blessed, then *leave it alone* for now at least. There's so much to be learned about stamps, and about the hobby, so rather than tear apart someone's old collection, live with it for a while. You might make decisions now you will regret later. Think of it as doing a huge crossword puzzle with an ink pen; it makes a lot of sense to read the whole thing through first, filling in words mentally. That way you can avoid indelible mistakes, although unlike crossword puzzles, with stamps there is no purely "right" or "wrong" way to do things. Mainly I am cautioning you not to make mistakes that will damage stamps or greatly diminish their value to other collectors.

So where *do* you find stamps? Well, someone else's discarded collection is a great place to start, although it certainly isn't the only way. In my own case, I started tearing through every drawer in my house, ripping stamps off every envelope and postcard I could find. My parents weren't amused, but eventually they got over it. And, after all, it *was* forgivable: sudden-onset stamp addiction; a child possessed. Besides, I didn't do too much damage.

It *was* wrong, of course. And I probably should have left the stamps on the envelopes—as I've said, they often are more valuable that way. Still, it was a start, and it kept me satisfied for many weeks, searching out stamps in closets, drawers, files, boxes. If you are just starting out, then begin your search for stamps right in your own home. Now obviously this suggestion doesn't mean that you should just tear through other people's personal belongings. Ask permission first: people who treasure old love letters may treasure them most when they are intact, with stamps still in place.

If you are like most stamp collectors, you fantasize constantly about uncovering that great, rare, incredibly valuable stamp that will not only get you noticed, but will also

A portion of a cover, showing the variety of unusual stamps issued by Tonga.

finance the rest of your hobby. It's kind of like buying lottery tickets, only with stamps, when you don't "win," you still have something of (relative) value.

The history of the hobby is rife with stories of old letters casually stuck in books, and when the books are then sold at secondhand stores for pennies, the letters are discovered and they bear stamps worth small fortunes. Okay, so most of these stories are apocryphal—still it's that great hope of finding something truly unusual, perhaps even rare, that keeps the devoted philatelist so passionate for the hobby.

So you are looking for stamps at home, ever vigilant, ever hopeful for something rare. In the meantime you simply take them *all*. So they look the same—no matter, since with stamps you never know. (In Chapter 5 you will see what I mean; several stamps may look identical, yet be distinct. It's one of the great challenges—as well as sources of fun—of the hobby.)

If you are one of the extremely lucky novice philatelists who lives in a big old house chock-full of closets filled with boxes and an attic stacked with dusty trunks, then you are indeed blessed. Territory such as that, especially if it is virgin and unexplored, is the stuff of dreams.

Go about your search carefully. Avoid the frenzy that may threaten, that urge to tear madly through everything, ripping the corners off every envelope you see. As I've said before—and will say repeatedly—envelopes left intact (known as "covers") often are more valuable than the individual stamp by itself, although this cautionary note pertains primarily to older stamps, say those generally issued prior to 1920. Later, when you know more about what you're doing, you can remove the stamps from the majority of these envelopes.

In addition to searching through your house, ask friends and relatives to search through their homes for stamps for you as well. You will be surprised how many people enjoy helping you; many of them may have been saving stamps, sticking them in a drawer or an envelope, just waiting for someone such as you to come along. If you're really lucky, you may even know someone who works for a company that conducts a lot of business with individuals or other companies overseas. Bank employees, for example, are frequently excellent sources for foreign stamps. Don't be hesitant about asking friends to save stamps for you; most will be happy to do it, and you may even be instrumental in getting one or two of them to begin collections of their own.

Which brings us to our next great source for stamps—other collectors. Now, stamp collecting is not necessarily the most sociable of hobbies; one does tend to spend hours alone, hunched over album pages, or sorting through great mounds of loose stamps. But it can be fun doing some of this sorting and searching with a friend, and it is especially fun when this friend has in his or her collection copies of stamps that you want. Trades are always in order, and chances are there are duplicates of many varieties in someone else's collection that will fit in nicely with your own.

Many people like to collect stamps featuring zeppelins. These are from Russia, circa 1936.

If you do live in a fairly densely populated area, there may well be a stamp club near you, or perhaps there is one in your school. Alas, they are not as common today as they once were—video junkies are frequently blind to the less animated joys of philately—but they do exist and are still quite popular.

When you do go to a stamp club, don't expect beer parties and secret handshakes—stamp collectors may individually be wild and crazy people, but as a group we appear and act conservatively. This is not to say, of course, that we are not well-rounded, absolutely fascinating individuals, but the key word is "individual"—philatelists tend to be very much their own persons. Maybe that is why stamp clubs tend to be businesslike, no-nonsense operations where people talk about their collections, their finds, their discoveries. And where stamps are swapped.

When it comes to trading stamps, follow your own instincts. As you will learn later (Chapter 4), there is a way of determining the relative catalogue value of every postal stamp ever issued. Once you have mastered the intricacies of valuation, you will be able to make relatively even trades. Until then, however, it is best to trade only those stamps of which you have multiple copies. That way, you won't be giving away something of irreplaceable value.

Stamp Shows

When a collector first encounters the term "stamp show," he or she is likely to assume that it is a place or event where people show off their collections. To some extent, this is a correct assumption—at most stamp shows, there are displays of portions of individual collections, typically on a fairly narrow topic.

The main purpose of most stamp shows, however, is the opportunity they provide for stamp dealers from the area—and sometimes from much farther away—to set up tables and display their wares. On first entering a stamp show area, one is confronted with rows of tables piled with boxes and displays of stamps for sale. Some of the dealers handle only one area of interest—stamps from France and French possessions, for example—while others offer a whole range of items. Some sell individual stamps, while others sell accumulations of all sizes, perhaps even whole collections.

It helps to know what you are looking for when going to a large stamp show, because the sheer volume of material available can be daunting. If you are just there to "look around," then there is plenty of opportunity, and if you want to buy wholesale lots of stamps to sort through later, you should find a substantial supply. But if individual stamps are your goal, then by all means take a "want list" with you; compare the prices at different tables, and be prepared to bargain— you will be surprised how many dealers are ready to negotiate a final sales price.

In addition to the collections on display, and the array of stamps and related items for sale, stamp shows also offer an excellent opportunity to get to know other collectors and to establish relationships with dealers. These men and women are for the most part extremely knowledgeable about all aspects of the hobby, and you may well find someone who is willing to keep an eye out for particular types of items or collections you may want to acquire.

To find out when and where these stamp shows take place, check with an area stamp club or consult the "Stamp Events Calendar" in *Linn's Stamp News* or one of the other stamp weeklies. The majority of these events are on a relatively small scale, held over a weekend in a hotel conference room. Others are much larger, however, and may require travel to larger cities where there are convention centers. When you go, be prepared to spend plenty of time and only as much money as you can afford. Chances are you will find much to tempt you.

CHEAP AT HALF THE PRICE

Once you have all your relatives, and all your friends, and all their friends and relatives searching out stamps for you; once you have pawed through the collections of all your friends—where do you turn for more stamps?

Back when people smoked cigarettes, and it was okay

to advertise your wares on match covers, it seemed like every other pack of cigarettes came with a book of matches that carried an advertisement exhorting you to send ten cents to the address given and they would in turn send you twenty-five all different, worldwide stamps. (Actually, you still see these advertisements on match books, only not so often and definitely not for ten cents.) Most of these outfits were (and still are) totally reputable; true to their word, you got your twenty-five stamps. And you immediately hungered for more.

That was when you returned the enclosed form that said that it was okay for them to send you more stamps "on approval." What they mean by "on approval" is that they send you stamps that you get to keep if you pay what they are asking. If you don't want those particular stamps, or if you think they are too expensive, then you return them. This method of viewing stamps on approval remains a common method of buying stamps, especially for collectors who live in areas where there are few stamp dealers.

With many dealers who sell on approval by mail, you can tell them your areas of special interest, and they will send you stamps corresponding to that interest. Say, for example, you want to see only French stamps, or if you have a topical collection and exclusively want stamps depicting horses, then you tell the dealer, and those will be the only stamps you see.

One word of caution regarding "approvals" is in order. Typically these dealers will send you stamps collectively valued at something less than fifty dollars, generally so that if something goes wrong with the postal service—it does happen you know, only never to bills—and the stamps are lost, the resulting loss is not too great financially. On these orders, the dealer normally doesn't go to the additional expense and trouble of insuring or registering the shipment. If you are nervous, however, then do return the unpurchased stamps either insured or in some way that requires a signed receipt. Under current regulations certified mail never carries any insurance coverage. You'll get a mailing receipt, and a signature showing the mail was received, if you pay for it. A less expensive way is to use a Return Receipt for Merchandise to achieve both goals. Also, if a dealer sends stamps that are too expensive, then stop doing business with him.

Stamp dealers are often also an excellent source of new material. They abound in larger metropolitan areas, but can be found just about anywhere. Look in the Yellow Pages of your local telephone directory, usually under the listing "Stamps for Collectors." Most of these dealers are collectors themselves, and they sometimes treat their stock as though it were a treasure you should have to beg to purchase.

This brings us to a question that has to be dealt with when purchasing stamps: what does one pay? This book's final chapter will deal extensively with the value of stamps and the value of your collection as a whole. It will also explain in detail the pricing system for stamps that is prevalent throughout the world. It is enough for now to say simply that you should follow your own instincts, and assess just how badly you want a particular stamp or set of stamps. And don't be afraid to bargain. In the true European tradition (or is it middle eastern?), one hardly ever expects to pay the asking price for stamps when dealing directly with a dealer. Always offer less. You may not get it for what you offer, but there's a good chance you will purchase it for less than the asking price.

With regard to dealers, if you are lucky enough to have a good dealer near you, then visit on a regular basis. Once you have determined your principal area of interest, and your collection is assuming a shape of some sort, the dealer can be on the lookout for items you may want or need. He also may be an excellent source for raw collections, those volumes and boxes of stamps found in attics or stuck in drawers, typically left behind when a young collector moves on to other pursuits. These collections are frequently sold by parents to these dealers for just a few dollars. Now in most cases they may not be worth more than a few dollars, but it may still be a good way to expand your own collection by buying one that has been discarded. True, the dealer will mark up the price considerably from what he paid, but it still will be cheaper to purchase an unsorted collection as opposed to buying the same stamps one at a time, after the dealer has spent hours sorting through them, cataloging each stamp. And remember— who knows what undetected gem may lurk in that junky old album with all its pages falling out. Chances are you won't find anything special, but there's always the hope.

A good way to get to know stamp dealers in your area is to attend a regional stamp show. These affairs are typically held on weekends in the conference center of a local motel, and strictly speaking these affairs usually aren't really "shows" at all. What they are, however, is a place for area stamp dealers—and occasionally some from farther away—to congregate and to display their wares.

By visiting these shows you can get to know the dealers in your area. More importantly, they can get to know you, and to know just what you are looking for. With rare exceptions, these are totally trustworthy folks, perhaps slightly more eccentric than the people who sell small appliances at the local hardware store, but fine nonetheless.

In my own case, there are two or more dealers in my area who have become friends of sorts (we may not exchange intimate secrets, but we speak on the phone regularly, keep up to date, and occasionally make deals). In addition, through these area shows I have gotten on the mailing lists for other dealers, who regularly send me catalogues listing current items for sale. It's an excellent and painless way of keeping up with what's out there and what the current prices are. And every now and then I buy something.

Another way to purchase stamps from dealers is through mail order advertisements you will find in the various stamp publications. In these instances, dealers usually list individual stamps they have for sale, and the price at which they are offering them for sale. Ordering stamps in this way enables the collector to fill gaps, purchasing only those stamps wanted.

All these dealers, by the way, seem happy to accept personal checks in payment, although most will accept the usual credit cards as well. Ironically, they don't usually want to trade stamps for stamps. Barter of this kind is usually left to swaps among friends or club members.

One other popular way of purchasing stamps is through auctions. There are many outfits who do nothing but auction stamps both individually and in collections. Every now and then these transactions make headlines, like when some single stamp sells for some remarkably high price, or when government officials who are also stamp collectors use a federal limo and driver to go to an auction.

The larger auction houses which handle stamps exclusively often sell them in lots, and these lots can vary from one individual (and usually very rare) stamp to whole cartons of albums full of stamps. Ideally one gets to view the items before the auction, and also ideally one sets a value he or she feels is appropriate and then sticks with it. It is easiest if you are allowed only one "blind" bid whereby you declare the price you are willing to pay, and if someone bids higher, then so be it. In a live auction there is a tendency to get caught up in the frenzy and to just keep bidding. It's easy to pay too much that way.

Obviously, auctions are not ideal for novice collectors. It takes some savvy, some awareness of values, and a sense of the current market demand for the stamps of certain nations, to be able to participate successfully in an auction. Once you are more sophisticated about the hobby, however, auctions can be an excellent source of some of the harder-to-come-by items for a more reasonable price. And you can occasionally pick up whole collections at a relatively low per-stamp price.

The American Philatelic Society

Any stamp collector who intends to take the hobby seriously should consider joining the American Philatelic Society. It is the foremost philatelic organization in the United States, and it is an invaluable source of aid and information to all who join.

Among the many services the APS provides its members, the following are the most significant:

- The APS has an expertizing service available to all members. Included in the service is identification of difficult-to-identify stamps; an accurate catalogue valuation of stamps; and determination of forged and fake issues.
- The APS has a long established and nominally priced insurance program available to collectors. Among the options covered are fire damage and theft.
- The APS has a circuit book service that is offered to all members. It is essentially a stamps sales service in which members fill APS circuit books with stamps they want to sell, and these are sent out to members who have requested that they see stamps for sale from certain countries. Typically the prices in these circuit books are lower than one would get from a stamp dealer. They offer an excellent opportunity to fill gaps in albums at moderate prices.
- The APS has a large library of out-of-print philatelic publications that are made available to members upon request.
- *The American Philatelist* is a monthly magazine published by the APS and sent to all members as part of the regular membership. The publication contains articles of all varieties, many tending to be somewhat scholarly, but all of interest.

Membership in the APS is open to "all persons of good character" throughout the world. The fee for joining varies according to the type of membership you choose (regular, spouse, youth, etc.). For information on how to join, write to the American Philatelic Society, P.O. Box 8000, State College, PA 16803. And use a stamp on your letter; postage meters may be fine for businesses, but stamp collectors should always use stamps!

Another way of adding to your collection is by joining the American Philatelic Society and entering your name on their circuit routing lists. This means that you get a chance to purchase stamps that are offered for sale by other APS members. These stamps are displayed in circuit books, as they are called, which are routed to members several times a year. You simply purchase those stamps you want, then forward the books to the next name on the mailing list. Again, it is an opportunity to fill in gaps in your collection at reasonable prices. These circuits can also be tailored to fit your own individual interest, so that if, for example, you want to see only Russian stamps, then that's what you'll be sent.

In Chapter 4 we will deal in detail with the use of stamp catalogues. If you intend to collect with any degree of sophistication, then it is essential to master these volumes, although "master," I hasten to point out, means only learning how to read them and generally how to disregard the prices listed therein. Suffice it to say, once you know the simple procedure for looking up a particular stamp, you are basically home free, since you will see a price or value listed and can use that as your guide in determining what you should pay.

Total this page $ 44.55   Country 1

Cat. No. 231	Cat. Val. 18.00	Cat. No. 232	Cat. Val. 12.50	Cat. No. 237	Cat. Val. 5.50
1 Net $ 9.00		2 Net $ 6.25		3 Net $ 2.75	
Cat. No. 234	Cat. Val. 6.50	Cat. No. 285	Cat. Val. 3.75	Cat. No. 287	Cat. Val. 16.00
4 Net $ 3.25		5 Net $ 1.85		6 Net $ 8.00	
Cat. No. 294	Cat. Val. 2.50	Cat. No. 295	Cat. Val. .75	Cat. No. 330	Cat. Val. 15.00
7 Net $ 1.25		8 Net $ .35		9 Net $ 7.50	
Cat. No. 370	Cat. Val. 1.50	Cat. No. 372	Cat. Val. 3.25	Cat. No. 397	Cat. Val. 11.00 No Gum
10 Net $ .75		11 Net $ 1.60		12 Net $ 2.00	

A typical page from an APS circuit book.

3

Housing Your Collection: Choosing the Best Way to Display Your Stamps

———

All right. By this time you've given some thought to what kind of a collection you are going to have, and you have assessed your own situation as to how best to get stamps. Let's assume, therefore, that you have this shoebox full of stamps sitting on a shelf. So what do you do with it?

One major consideration—in fact, *the* major consideration—in deciding which way to go in putting your stamps on pages is just what kind of collection you intend to have, or at least what your primary focus will be.

If you are going to collect stamps from the whole world, then you can go about selecting just about any album you may want, or you can choose from any number of alternatives to albums.

If you want to collect only one or two countries, then

there are some very sophisticated albums you can purchase, or, again, you can make your own.

With regard to topical collections, however, it becomes at the same time more problematic and simpler. It is problematic because with few exceptions, there are no albums designed specifically to house topical collections. It is simple because you *have* to make your own album.

But whether you purchase an album or create your own, you will be amazed at the variety of ways there are to house and display your collection, and just how sophisticated some of the albums are. And just how expensive some of them are, as well. Let's save the high-finance variety of album till the end, however, and start out with a more basic and economic way of housing your stamps.

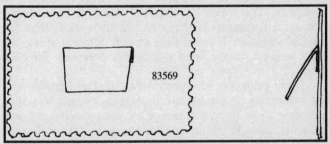

Stamp with a hinge attached.

First, however, a brief aside on how to put stamps on paper. There are two basic ways to get a stamp to stay on a sheet of paper: (1) stamp hinges, which are thin pieces of glassine paper with glue on one side, so that this piece of paper sticks at the same time to the stamp and to the page, affixed in a hingelike manner, thus the name; (2) any of the several other methods which allow the stamp to be displayed—usually through plastic protection—but in which no glue touches the stamp itself. These methods of display will be discussed in slightly more detail later, and are mentioned here because they are factors affecting which kind of album you may choose. Just remember that a collector never, never uses glue, scotch tape, or any fixative that will damage or destroy the stamp itself.

Just as I emphasized at the outset that your stamp collection is yours to shape in any way you want, there also are no rules when it comes to how you display it. The simplest way to display your stamps is to use a notebook with blank pages. This can be any kind of notebook, perhaps the kind used in schoolwork, with ruled pages. Or it can be a loose-leaf notebook, probably of the three-ring binder variety.

The benefits of a loose-leaf binder album include the important factor of being able to add pages at will and at any place. This would be of special benefit if, for example, you are collecting more than one country or more than one topical selection. If you collect several different areas, you may well eventually need a different notebook for each one.

Some collectors who prefer loose-leaf or flexible, add-on notebooks or albums, use blank pages which they then decorate or in some way design for their specific use, and in some cases these designs may become very elaborate. Again I emphasize that however you want to display your stamps is fine, so long as you don't destroy or damage them in the process. Some designed sheets enhance, while others get so ornate as to detract from the stamps themselves. It is, however, a matter of personal preference.

Obviously, such items as prebound scrapbooks and photo albums can function as well for display of stamps, although their pages are typically heavier than necessary. It is also generally best to use only white paper. Any colored paper could eventually bleed onto the stamps and cause discoloration which greatly diminishes the value of the stamp. Likewise, photo albums with adhesive backing and

A typical page from a homemade stamp album.

plastic overlay sheets are not desirable since stamps with gum may adhere permanently.

All these unstructured ways of displaying your collection have the advantage of allowing you to shape your collection in any way you choose, and it is, I think, the best way for a novice collector to begin. If you organize your stamps in whatever way you decide—by country, by topic, by year, and so forth—you can then simply mount them in the notebook/album. Then later, when you are a little more sophisticated about philately, you may decide to purchase one of the several kinds of specialized albums available through stamp dealers, catalogues, and some few department stores.

Before going into a discussion of some of the albums available to collectors, it's worth mentioning another method of housing and displaying your stamps that gives you the flexibility of shaping and organizing your collection in any way you choose.

Stock books consist of heavy paper or cardboard pages that have rows of plastic or paper strips or pockets. Stamps can be slipped into these pockets and are kept in place without the need for hinges. On stock pages with plastic pockets, the stamps are fully visible; on those made entirely of cardboard, most stamps project far enough above the strip to be distinguished. These pages give you total flexibility in organizing your stamps, and provide protection for them as well. The major disadvantage is that they are expensive, or at least are much more costly than your basic notebook pages. They also are available generally only at stamp supply stores.

If you decide to start a worldwide collection, there are many, many different albums and kinds of albums available to you. Some are basic and relatively inexpensive; others are quite sophisticated and cost a small fortune.

A personal recollection seems appropriate here. When I was first collecting, after I had tired of sticking—with stamp hinges, always with stamp hinges—my stamps in

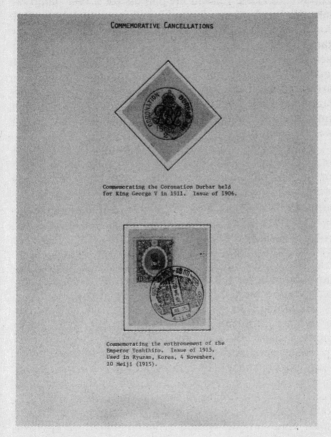

COMMEMORATIVE CANCELLATIONS

Commemorating the Coronation Durbar held
for King George V in 1911. Issue of 1906.

Commemorating the enthronement of the
Emperor Yoshihito. Issue of 1915.
Used in Ryuzan, Korea, 4 November,
10 Meiji (1915).

Some people create their own special album pages using only a pen
and a typewriter.

school notebooks, I asked my parents for a real stamp album. By "real stamp album," I had in mind a book that would have places for all my stamps. Well, they got me a stamp album all right, a worldwide album that came with pictures of national flags and brief descriptions of each country's geography and history. The album wasn't particularly large, but I was very proud of it. Now instead of blank pages that I filled helter-skelter, here were pages with pictures of actual stamps, and I was to stick the real stamps over the picture.

So far so good. The only problem was, all these pictures were of stamps I didn't have. And there were actual places for only a fraction of the stamps I did have. What was going on? I wondered: were my stamps so rare as to not require places in so basic an album? Unfortunately, no. This simply was not a very good album. It offered a few pages for each country, all right, but little reasoning seemed to have gone into deciding which stamps to picture. In fact, the stamps in my collection were among the most common for the countries they came from, and certainly there should have been places for them.

Thumbing through my virtually empty album gave rise to another problem. I didn't want to see those pages empty. I wanted those stamps—all of them. I wanted to fill up those pages. And that's when I started buying stamps. *Really* buying stamps, by putting all my allowance money toward packets of stamps I could find at the dime store (okay, so we are talking ancient history). Woolworth was good for only so many varieties of stamps; I wanted still more. That's when I started ordering stamps on approval through the mails.

But buy as I might, those blank pages continued to mock me. So finally I gave up. Just quit. Put my stamps and my hateful empty album into a drawer. Confessed to my father that a stamp dealer who claimed I had kept some stamps without paying for them was threatening to garnishee my wages and take away my car (enough to strike

An album stock page with stamps arranged according to Scott catalogue number.

terror in the heart of any twelve year old). And directed my energies elsewhere (also natural for a twelve-year-old boy).

In the years that followed, I never forgot about my fledgling stamp collection, and I kept squirreling away foreign stamps as I found them. Finally, years later, on a visit home, I retrieved it. And I started all over again. Wiser—much, much wiser—but every bit as dedicated.

So I guess the moral of this little story is, *no album* is better than *the wrong album*. So how do you recognize the "wrong album"? And what constitutes a "right album"?

Obviously, for me the wrong album was one that presented an unrealistic challenge. It was a survey album, offering places for random stamps from virtually all nations, extending from the earliest stamps of each country up to the most recent. This approach is basically okay and is used in a lot of popular world survey albums. The problem with my album was that virtually all the pages were crammed with pictures of stamps, one or two from each year, and there were almost no blank spots where I could add those stamps that weren't pictured.

A better album of this sort will picture several of the most common stamps from the earlier years and then leave ample blank space for others that the collector may have found. These albums consist typically of a kind of loose-leaf binder so that supplemental pages can be added at will. Such an album is best for beginning collectors, I think. It contains enough pictures of stamps, covering all major definitive issues, and spanning the years, yet it allows the collector either blank spaces to add those less common stamps he or she may have found, or it allows for the addition of entire blank pages on which to display stamps not featured on album pages.

One of the great problems with survey albums is that in the last couple of decades, the output of stamps in virtually every nation has increased dramatically, and providing spaces for even a sampling of these issues becomes almost impossible.

Another problem with survey albums is that they have gotten very expensive, and for the collector just starting out and unsure of what direction to take, buying an expensive album that will later be discarded can be a waste. For example, H. E. Harris—one of the oldest company names in the stamp business—offers a variety of worldwide survey albums. Now admittedly their cheapest entry—a paperbound album that only hints at the number of nations and stamps out there—is something called the *Explorer Child Album,* and it catalogues for a mere $3.95. The album is a fine way to tantalize a child, to perhaps interest him in the hobby, or to see if her proclaimed intent to collect stamps is merely a whim. If it is anything more than a whim, the *Explorer* will soon be discarded for something more satisfying.

Harris offers a variety of other worldwide albums, with cost varying according to number of pages, illustrations, and binding. The true "beginner's" album is one called the *Traveler* that offers space for approximately 10,000 stamps and contains illustrations for some 4,000; it catalogues for $19.95. The *Traveler* will keep a beginning collector occupied for a while, but it too will eventually prove inadequate for a truly serious collector.

At the top of Harris's list of worldwide albums is a four-volume set that breaks the world down into four geographical areas. The company advertises that the set contains room for more than 175,000 different stamps, and provides some 100,000 illustrations of same. And while 175,000 sounds like a lot of stamps, the albums still would not be complete in offering room for all issues; they should, however, suffice for most collectors. The retail price? A mere $275.00 for the four-volume set. See what I mean? It gets very expensive.

So what do you do?

Well, if you think you want to collect worldwide, I'd

A typical page from one of the less expensive Harris albums.

suggest you start with something simple like the *Traveler*. That way, if you find you want to specialize in one area or one country, you won't have invested too much money in an album you will discard. You may well find that you will want to revert to one of the other ways of housing your stamps we covered earlier. Printed albums such as the *Traveler* provide the collector with barebone outlines of the philatelic world, and offer some framework on which to structure the collection, but they are limited and limiting. Creating your own album once you are truly familiar with the particular country and its stamps can be a fascinating next step.

I must point out here that by no means is H. E. Harris the only company that offers worldwide survey albums for collectors, nor is it necessarily the best. There are not, however, the wide variety of albums for sale there once were. A number of factors have contributed to this unfortunate situation: inflation, MTV, Arnold Schwarzenegger movies. The Minkus company offers a couple of survey entries, the more basic being the *New World Wide Album* with spaces for over 25,000 stamps, including 16,000 illustrations. The catalogue price is $34.95 At the high—very high—end of the range for worldwide albums is the Scott International Series. It is certainly the most comprehensive set of its kind, arranging entries from all nations in chronological order. As of this writing, there are thirty-seven separate volumes in the set, and the set retails for $3,380.00. Each volume in the set covers a specific period of time and arranges all countries in alphabetical order. And while there is not room for every single stamp issued (this is true especially in the earliest years), it is a very impressive set. Obviously not for the beginner, it is something only the most dedicated collector would attempt to tackle. One other factor to keep in mind: the Scott International Series takes up almost twelve feet of shelf space.

As I mentioned earlier, there are few albums offered for collectors of topicals. Among those I have encountered is an album which promises to offer space for all stamps issued featuring Disney characters (more of these have been issued than you would believe possible). Obviously, one of the complicating factors in the area of topicals is that the album must account for stamps issued by *all* countries. For this reason there are fewer prepared and illustrated albums covering topicals. Smaller albums—some of them issued by the U.S. Post Office in an effort to stimulate interest in philately—covering such areas as black heritage and sports are also available, but these are strictly for novices.

If you have decided to focus on stamps from the United States, there are many albums from which to choose. Harris once again offers one of the best basic albums for collectors—the *Liberty Album*. It is virtually complete, fully illustrated, and relatively durable. The price, while not cheap, is reasonable (current catalogue price is $39.95), especially when compared to the competition. Ka-Be, for example, offers an extremely fine set of pages—pages only, no binder—for $293.50. Lighthouse offers U.S. pages and binder, complete, all issues, for $687.00. Scott offers pages only for $69.95; the binder sells for approximately $25.00.

So as you can see, for collectors of U.S. stamps there is a wide range of choices. The differences in prices derive primarily from such things as the quality of the paper used, the number of pages used—Lighthouse, for example, typically has space for only a very few stamps per page, allowing for excellent display—and the quality of the illustrations and the printing. All suppliers offer annual supplements for sale, so that if you bought an album in 1993, it might include pages for all stamps issued through 1992, and you would then buy annual supplements providing space for all stamps issued thereafter.

And what if you want to specialize in stamps from countries other than the United States? What if you want to concentrate on collecting stamps from, say, Great Britain or Japan, or maybe from some of the emerging African nations? We've dealt elsewhere with where to find the stamps. What about specialized albums for individual countries? Unfortunately, this is where the hobby can get most expensive.

Let's take France as an example and look at the various philatelic suppliers to see what it might cost to house a specialized French collection. Scott offers complete pages (in all cases, complete pages for France cover the years 1849–1989) for $101.85. Minkus lists complete pages for $82.50, while the minimum cost from Lighthouse would be $257.00. And from Ka-Be the retail figure for complete pages would be a whopping $348.15.

Add to these figures the cost for binders, and you have made a major investment without even thinking about the purchase of stamps themselves. As you can see, casual stamp collecting utilizing classroom-type notebooks is one thing. Highly specialized philately is quite another. Both are equally enjoyable, or so I think. It really is a matter of how obsessive you become about the hobby. Use reason and proceed at a leisurely pace. I know that when I took up the hobby after some years away, I quickly started expanding and found myself rather rapidly in debt and more than a little overwhelmed by the sheer volume of material I had accumulated.

A word of advice if you do decide to focus your collection on one or two countries. A good way to get both stamps *and* a suitable specialized album is to purchase someone else's collection. This was discussed somewhat in the proceeding chapter, but now that you have a sense of just how expensive the specialized album can be, you see just how great a bargain someone else's collection might be, especially if both pages and binder are in good condition.

Another relevant factor to consider at this point, and one which was a major point in my own decision to use Scott albums exclusively, is the manner in which stamps are given individual, designated numbers. The recognized au-

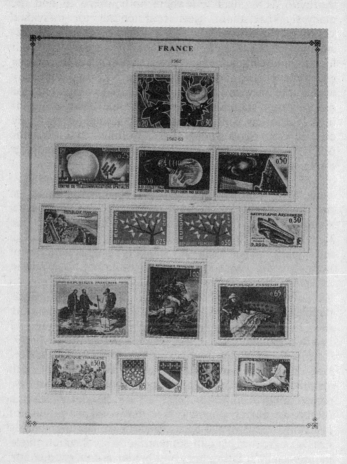

A typical page from the Scott International Album.

thority on U.S. philately is the Scott company. For many, many years, Scott has been recording each new issue of stamps by the United States Postal Service. Scott has studied these issues, accounting for announced variations and looking for anything unannounced that might cause stamps which otherwise appear to be identical to in fact be different issues. As we will cover later, there are many minor differences in stamps which might cause these distinguishing designations. Suffice it for now to say simply that they exist and that Scott studies them carefully and gives a different catalogue number to each and every stamp. As a result, Scott is the recognized authority on U.S. stamps and on U.S. postal history as well.

Scott albums are keyed to these numbers, and its specialized albums contain places for every single stamp to which it has given a designated number. In addition, Scott has also set a value on each stamp, in both used and mint conditions, and most U.S. stamp dealers use the Scott catalogue value as a reference point when establishing cost or valuation.

For these reasons, Scott would seem to be the album of choice, at least for U.S. collections. While Scott also has given number designations to stamps issued by virtually all other countries, it is by no means necessarily the authority on stamps of these countries. The stamps of Great Britain, for example, are remarkably complex, yet are given rather shallow treatment in the Scott catalogue for that country. For all British stamps—U.K. and Commonwealth—Stanley Gibbons, a British company, is the recognized authority. This doesn't mean that the Scott catalogue for Great Britain isn't valid and useful, and that the Scott album for that country isn't adequate, but if you were planning to specialize in stamps of Great Britain, you would want to use only the best sources in establishing your collection.

So you see how complex—and expensive—the simple act of housing your stamp collection can become. There's no point in reviewing all the options open to you. Just remember that this hobby is all about enjoying yourself and enjoying the collecting of stamps. You can do it as simply as you like; there is no absolute right or wrong way to do any of it.

4

Mastering the Technical
Aspects of Stamp Collecting

—

Up to this point we have dealt with the basics of collecting
stamps—what they are, where to find them, and how to
display them. In this chapter, and the two following, we
will be concerned with slightly more complex considerations. First we will cover the basic technical information
and the most common terminology you will encounter. The
goal is to provide a substantial working knowledge of the
various components of collecting, so that you will be able
to decipher advertisement of stamps for sale as well as
catalogue descriptions. At the end of this chapter, we will
look in detail at a couple of typical entries from the Scott
catalogues. In the next chapter, we will look at all the—
sometimes confusing—aspects of stamp condition. Following that, we will review the tools and ancillary materials

Definitive stamps issued in the United States in 1917–1919, as displayed in the Scott U.S. Album.

important in maintaining your collection, as well as the basics of caring for and storing your stamps.

For purposes of easy reference, whenever possible I will present this basic information in the form of alphabetical mini-glossaries. I'd suggest, however, that initially you read straight through all these separate entries. Hopefully that way you will see how these various elements interrelate and perhaps will find the logic in what initially may seem to be an overly complicated system of classification and distinction. For a hobby that in its most basic form is really just about gathering little pieces of paper, stamp collecting can at times seem overwhelmingly complicated. Let's see if we can do something to demystify and to simplify things.

A LOOK AT THE STAMP ITSELF

This stamp—a little piece of paper—is actually a thing of many parts. A basic familiarity with the terms used in describing a stamp, and an understanding of how these terms are used, is important to anyone interested in philately. If you intend to pursue the hobby seriously, then this familiarity is essential.

Paper: There are a variety of papers that historically have been used in the manufacture of stamps. You will need to have a working understanding of the most basic types, for their names will appear with some regularity in catalogue descriptions of stamps and sometimes may be the sole distinguishing factor between two otherwise identical stamps.

The two basic types of paper used in the manufacture of stamps are *wove* and *laid*. The easiest way to distinguish between them is visual, by looking at a stamp when held against a light. When the surface of the paper is smooth, and the texture appears uniform, with no light or dark areas evident, it is said to be "wove." (This texture is created in the manufacturing process, as the wet fibers are intertwined or woven together before drying.) When this paper is held to the light, you can see little dots very close together. "Laid" paper, on the other hand, when held to the light, will reveal alternating light and dark lines, and the paper may have a slightly ridged or textured feeling to the touch. (As with wove, laid paper is a result of the manufacturing process, wherein a wire screen with lines of alternating thickness produce a paper of similar lined effect.) Generally speaking, the greatest number of stamps are printed on wove paper.

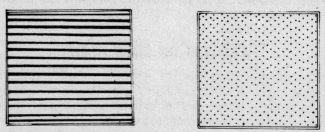

Two types of paper as they would appear when wet. On the left is laid paper and on the right, wove.

There are numerous variations of paper that historically have been used in the manufacture of stamps. Some of the additional kinds you are likely to encounter include:

Granite—the paper is filled with short fibers of many different colors.

Pelure—a thin and often very brittle or hard paper, frequently grayish in shade.

Quadrille—the lines in the paper when held to the light form little squares.

One other distinction about paper you should keep in mind is that some varieties are created in shades other than white, in which case both the front and back of the stamp will be in that shade. The same effect is sometimes created by printing the front with a solid color before the design is applied, but the back remains white. These differences are easy to detect, but you must remember to look for them.

Ink: While a variety of inks have been used in the production of stamps, it is not necessary to have any special knowledge of them in order to survive as a philatelist. There are apparently some inks that may wash out of stamps when soaked, but I, fortunately, have not encountered any of them, and chances are you won't either. It is a good idea, however, whenever handling older stamps—and especially those that are more valuable—to read all information you can find about them. That way you can avoid any costly and damaging mistakes.

Color: While ink may not be a critical consideration for the average stamp collector, the color of that ink often presents a challenge to even the most experienced among us. In many instances, color can be the sole factor in determining differences between stamps that are otherwise identical, and for collectors of some countries—especially those concentrating on the United States—these color differences can be very important. And incredibly frustrating. Some of these color distinctions are so difficult to make out that one may be tempted to toss a coin in deciding, for example, whether something is bluish green or greenish blue. It actually gets that ridiculous at times, and I truly wonder in many of these cases if the great god of philately isn't pulling our collective leg. Nonetheless, one perseveres, using a handy color guide (see Chapter 6), hoping to be right at least most of the time. Confusing things even further is the fact that sometimes these distinctions are dismissed as "shade variations," due—one must assume—to printing sloppiness. As a seasoned stamp collector, I find color the most baffling and irritating part of what nonetheless remains an absolutely fascinating hobby.

Printing process: Another distinguishing characteristic that at times can be somewhat confusing, the various printing processes used in the manufacture of stamps at least don't offer the confounding challenge you get with color distinctions. Occasionally you will come upon stamps that are identical in design, color, and paper, but that are listed as different stamps in catalogues because they have been printed by different processes. With some exceptions, once you are familiar with the basic differences between these methods of printing, you will be able to distinguish these different varieties with the naked eye.

There are several basic methods of printing that will concern you:

Engraving: Stamps described as engraved have been printed from plates in which the image or design has been etched into metal, and ink then fills in the recesses. When the paper is pressed against the metal plate, enough pressure is applied to force the paper into these recessed areas; the ink adheres to the paper and typically creates a raised effect on the surface which can be felt by running a finger over the stamp. Virtually all U.S. stamps issued prior to 1960 were engraved.

Photogravure: Similar to engraving in terms of the process, except since no special pressure is applied to the paper during the printing, photogravure does not result in a raised surface and is distinguished under magnification by the dot structure of the ink on the paper, which should appear as a mass of evenly spaced fine dots of the same size.

Typography: This method of printing is essentially the opposite of engraving. Here the ink is applied to a design that is raised above the surface of the plate. As a result, there is no effect of raised ink on the face of the stamp, and often the design may be distinguished by depressed areas on the stamp, similar to the effect produced by a typewriter.

Lithography: Also known as *offset* printing, lithography is easily the most common method of printing employed generally today—virtually all book and most magazines and catalogues (and junk mail) are printed in this way. Lithography has been used increasingly in the printing of stamps as well. One need only look at the change from the more common one-color stamps produced by most countries up until the 1960s to the elaborate four-color varieties frequently used today—this change is due in great part to the development of offset printing. Lithographed stamps have smooth surfaces and are typically printed on smooth-surfaced paper.

Embossing: Technically not a "printing" process—no ink need be used in embossing—an embossed stamp has had an impression forced into the paper in such a way that the design is raised well above the surface, and can easily be detected. Most postal stationery is embossed.

Watermarks: Not the most difficult distinction you will encounter as a stamp collector, watermarks nonetheless present a challenge that can be quite frustrating at times. They appear as dark designs or patterns within the paper itself, and were incorporated into the production of stamps primarily in an effort to thwart counterfeiting. It would take more knowledge than you need of the entire paper manufacturing process in order to fully comprehand how watermarks are created. It's enough that you understand that they are actually thin spots in the paper and that many can be seen by the unaided eye; those that can't are usually detected through use of watermark fluid or by placing the stamps in special contraptions created solely for use by philatelists. Watermark detection is important because frequently the presence of a watermark in a stamp's paper, or the use of different watermarks, may be the only feature distinguishing otherwise identical stamps. Watermark detection becomes difficult when two or more watermarks are very similar, or when the quality of the paper itself is inferior and a number of unintentional thin spots can be seen. (Also, just about any yellow or orange stamp poses a special problem in accurately detecting a watermark.) Watermarks are generally described in the Scott's catalogues, with visual examples of each. In time you will become relatively adept at detecting these designs, and you may actually come to enjoy this part of the hobby. At times, however, it can seem primarily tedious and thankless and irritating, even to a seasoned collector. My advice on them is simply to do the best you can, and when in doubt as to which watermark you are looking at, opt for the one that is the more common.

The physical stamp, beyond the paper and its watermark, and the ink and its color, is made up of a number of parts. Unlike color distinctions and occasionally watermarks, these parts are generally precise and consistent throughout the entire range of international philately and are relatively easy to distinguish.

The entire area of artwork on the face of the stamp is known as the *design*. Only occasionally will this artwork extend from one edge of the stamp to the other. More typically there is an unprinted border around the design; this part of the stamp is call the *margin*. Some stamps may have a line of color between the design and the margin known as the *frame*. A clear and distinct, well-centered design and evenly spaced margins are always desirable.

Another term you may encounter that deals with the physical stamp is *selvage*. This is the paper attached to the stamp—but which is not a part of it—that is actually a piece of the entire *pane* or *sheet* of stamps as it is initially sold at the post office. There may be printing on the selvage, and some collectors place a high value on stamps with selvage attached.

Two typical watermarks. The one at the top is an early watermark found in U.S. issues; the bottom one is from the earliest issues of Australia.

The back of the stamp is usually covered with *gum* that is moistened in order to make the stamp adhere. Gum that is undisturbed—no part of its surface has been moistened or otherwise altered—is valued at a premium. (In the next chapter we will deal in some detail with this increasingly significant requirement among collectors that the gum side of a mint stamp be as pristine as the front.) Some older stamps were issued without gum, and there is an increasing tendency toward the use of new self-adhesive stamps in some countries. The United States has tried self-adhesive stamps (covered with fast adhesive that will stick firmly to virtually any surface once the protective waxy paper backing has been peeled off), but has backed away from putting many of them on the market. Such stamps won't soak off envelopes and are very difficult to handle, so are not much in favor with collectors.

In some U.S. postal issues of the nineteenth century (most specifically for a ten-year period from 1860–1870, and then only on a limited number of stamps, as part of an experiment) the stamps were impressed with a *grill*. Basically this is a pattern of little holes which allowed the cancellation ink to penetrate that much farther into the paper. This was done in order to prevent reuse of stamps by washing off the ink. Because grills were used experimentally, not many issues had them and as a result they are generally quite rare. And because they are rare—and therefore more valuable—many fake grilled stamps have been created since the issues first appeared. It is very difficult to distinguish between genuine and fake grills, so it is best to ask for expert advice before investing in stamps of this type.

One final physical distinction you must be able to make in identifying otherwise identical stamps is the difference between *perforations*. Perforations are those tiny little holes punched in the paper that allow you to separate one stamp from another. Stamps that come in sheets with no perforations, and which must be cut apart, are said to be *imperforate*. Stamps that *are* perforated may be perforated in a variety of ways. The most common perforations are those in which evenly spaced holes border the stamp. *Roulette perforations* appear more as dashes than holes, while *serrate perforations* have a jagged, more irregular design. Generally these distinctions can be made with ease. Slightly more complex, although not so difficult that it can be tedious, is the determination of perforation sizes. Fortunately, a perforation gauge was developed many years ago that effectively serves to measure these various sizes. (See Chapter 6.) The numbers referred to as "sizes" are actually the number of perforation holes that fall in a space of two centimeters (or twenty millimeters). Thus, a stamp that is said to be "perf 10" ("perf" being the popular abbreviation for perforation) is one that has ten perforation holes in the space of two centimeters. Don't sweat this technical part of stamp examination—the perforation gauge is easy to use and seldom confusing. As I said initially, the greatest problem comes from the tedium of having to check the perforations on a large number of stamps.

Perforations.

DISTINGUISHING BETWEEN DIFFERENT TYPES OF STAMPS AND DIFFERENT AREAS OF COLLECTING

Some of the terms that follow may already be familiar. You may have encountered them earlier in the course of discussions concerning the various kinds of collecting one may pursue. Others will be repeated later in slightly different context. I include them here in the form of a glossary as a handy reference tool. Most of these terms are so rudimentary that if you have a reasonable level of familiarity with the hobby, you will be able to skim much of this material; others are slightly less basic, and you may want to refer back to them when you encounter them in the course of pursuing the hobby.

Airmails: Stamps issued for use on letters to be carried by air, airmails represent a distinct area of philately. Most countries traditionally have issued fewer airmail stamps than regular postal stamps, and many philatelists specialize in collecting them.

Back of the book: Also known as B-O-B, this term "back of the book" refers to the groupings of stamps that traditionally follow regular issues in the stamp catalogues. These areas include postage due stamps, special delivery stamps, newspaper stamps, official stamps, postal tax stamps, and a variety of other more limited areas of issue.

Bisect: Not a common situation, a bisect is a stamp that has been cut in half, appropriately enough for use when the postal rate calls for only half the value of the complete, uncut stamp. Because such a use has not been frequently allowed (if a five-cent postal rate is called for, generally a five-cent stamp is available, and ten-cent stamps bisected are not allowed), for a bisect to have full catalogue value, it usually must still be on at least a portion of the envelope (cover).

Block: A group of stamps at least two high and two across is called a block. Some collectors make a specialty of collecting blocks, especially those with plate numbers attached. (See Plate blocks.)

Booklet pane: Many more commonly used stamps are issued for sale in booklets, typically of two or more "panes" of stamps. These panes usually consist of six or eight or occasionally more stamps, and some collectors put a premium on whole booklet panes including selvage (an unprinted strip of paper attached to the stamps).

Bull's-eye: A postal cancellation that is centered more or less entirely on the stamp. Also known as "socked-on-the-nose," stamps with bull's-eye cancellations represent an area of specialized collecting very popular today.

Cachet: This term refers to the printing of a design on the left side of an envelope (cover), typically on a first day cover. This design usually is a thematic representation of the stamp also featured on the envelope, and may at times be quite elaborate. The cachets are printed solely for philatelic purposes and have nothing to do with the delivery of the mails.

Coils: Beginning in the early years of the twentieth century, there was a demand for stamps issued in bulk and in an easily used or dispensed form. The answer has been stamps issued in roll form, with the upper and lower edges of the stamps being straight, and perforations falling only between the stamps. These stamps are called coils.

Commemoratives: Commemorative stamps are those issued generally for sale for a limited period of time, and which carry a design featuring and commemorating some person, thing, or event, as compared to definitives or regular issues.

Cover: A cover is any envelope designed for postal use, or that has been postally used.

Cut square: On preprinted postal stationery the corner on which a stamp would ordinarily be placed is filled by a postal design printed directly on the envelope, and frequently embossed. When the corner of the envelope containing this design is cut away from the rest of the cover, the result is a cut square. Many philatelists include cut squares in their collections, an area especially popular among those specializing in U.S. issues.

Definitives: Regular issues of stamps, sold over a long period of time, are known as definitive stamps, or definitives. These stamps generally are issued in groups or sets, with similar designs on each stamp. These sets typically consist of stamps of many different denominations, ranging from lower values to much higher. (See Commemoratives.)

Essay: An essay is a proposed stamp design, but not one that was finally accepted and put into use.

Exploded: When a postal stamp booklet has been broken apart into its component panes, it is said to be exploded.

Fiscal: When a stamp is used for revenue or tax purposes, it is said to be a fiscal, or to be fiscally used. Fiscal use most commonly can be detected by the cancellation, which typically is a pen cancellation.

Franked: When a stamp has been used to pay the postage, it is said to frank a cover. Free franking would refer to postal use that requires no stamps.

Gutter pair: When two stamps are attached by an unprinted piece of paper between them, they are said to be a gutter pair. Such a production process has not

Examples of envelope cut squares and of an intact postal envelope. These are from Honduras in the 1890s.

been used extensively, and many gutter pairs are quite valuable.

Line pair: In strips of coil stamps, when a colored line (typically the same color ink as that of the stamp's design) appears between two stamps, these stamps constitute a line pair. This line is created by ink collecting in the space between two plates. Frequently, line pairs sell at a premium.

Mint: A stamp that has never been postally used and that is in the same condition it was when purchased at the post office is described as mint.

Multiple: Multiple refers to any grouping of more than one of the same stamp when they still are attached to each other, as they appeared when first issued.

Officials: Official stamps are issued exclusively for use by government departments on what is termed official mail.

Off paper: Off paper is a descriptive term typically used in advertisements of stamps for sale. It refers quite simply to stamps—in nearly all cases used and canceled—that have been soaked off the envelopes to which they were attached.

Overprint: Occasionally a printed stamp may be altered by the addition of words or symbols or even a new value. These additions are called overprints, typically issued when there is insufficient time to design and print a whole new stamp needed for some special reason. (See Surcharge.)

Pair: Two stamps still attached to each other as they were when issued constitute a pair.

Pane: The sheets of stamps that are sold at a post office are called panes by philatelists.

Plate block: A block of stamps (usually four copies) that has a plate number printed on the selvage attached to the block. Many collectors make a specialty of these.

Plate number: In the stamp production process, a control number is printed on the otherwise blank paper (see Selvage) attached to the stamp. This plate number is valued at a premium by many collectors.

An overprint.

Postage due: When a piece of mail is sent with insufficient postage affixed, the post office typically requires the addressee to pay the additional postage due. Most countries have issued postage due stamps for use in such instances.

Postal card: Postal cards are purchased directly from the post office. As with postcards, postal cards have a place for the sender to write a message, but unlike postcards, they come as well with a stamp already printed on the upper right-hand corner.

Postal stationery: Postal stationery refers to any embossed stamped envelope or postal card sold through the post office.

Postcard: Distinct from a *postal card,* a postcard is a card —often with a picture on one side—on which one may write a message and must place a stamp before putting it in the mail.

Postmark: Used as part of the cancellation when a piece of stamped mail is processed through the postal system, a postmark is a marking that traditionally indicates the city of cancellation (not always the same as the place of origin), the date, and occasionally even the hour of cancellation. A clear, distinct postmark may at times be of assistance in distinguishing between stamps that appear to be identical (early Austrian issues, for example), or occasionally it may help in determining the country of origin. (Early French stamps without a colonial overprint were sometimes used to post mail from French colonies, and the only way to determine such use is through the postmark.)

Postmaster provisionals: Prior to the time the U.S. Post Office began to issue its own stamps (see Chapter 7), some regional postmasters created their own stamps that were used on mail originating from their post offices, and occasionally when regular issues of stamps were in short supply. These postmaster provisionals are relatively rare and are prized by collectors.

Precancels: Not to be confused with stamps "canceled to order" (see Chapter 5 where both CTOs and precancels are discussed), precancels are stamps that are canceled prior to being put on a piece of mail. Such stamps are generally prepared for use in handling bulk mail.

Proof: A proof is a trial printing of a stamp, using the final design decided upon for the actual issue. Proofs occasionally are run in black ink, but often are in full color. These items are valued by many collectors.

Examples of precancels. Many philatelists make a specialty of collecting these, often concentrating on stamps from their own state or town.

Regular issue: This is another term for definitive stamps, sometimes used interchangeably. (See Definitives.)

Reissue: When a stamp that has been taken out of circulation, and is no longer being printed, is reprinted officially —by the postal service—it is known as a reissue. Occasionally, minor changes are made in the original design. (See Reprint, Chapter 5.)

Revenue: Revenues (discussed at some length in Chapter 1 and mentioned again here for easy reference) are stamps issued for the purpose of taxation and are required on certain legal papers and on products that are considered luxuries or which are regulated. Most medicines once required revenue stamps, as did more everyday items such as playing cards and boxes of matches. Cigarettes and other tobacco products demanded revenue stamps as well. These stamps are generally unique in appearance and are not likely to be confused with regular postal issues. Other revenue stamps, such as those for use on legal documents— stock certificates, deeds, etc.—are more similar to traditional postal stamps. In some countries, most notably Great Britain and many of its colonies, stamps for many years were issued for use interchangeably between postal and revenue purposes. Distinguishing between these uses is sometimes one of the great challenges of philately.

Semipostals: Semipostal issues are stamps that have two values printed on them: one value represents the amount paid to the post office, the other goes to charity. The United States has never issued semipostal stamps, but most other countries have.

Set: When a group of stamps are issued bearing similar designs, but usually different denominations, they are considered to be a set.

Se-tenant: Most commonly, stamps are issued in panes in which all the stamps are identical. Occasionally, however, stamps of different design are issued in the same pane. Attached stamps of different design are said to be se-tenant.

Souvenir sheet: Usually issued specifically for collectors, souvenir sheets are small panes of stamps with special commemorative designations. Because these sheets are

Revenue stamps come in a variety of sizes.

An example of se-tenant stamps.

much larger than individual stamps, they are seldom actually used for postal purposes and as a result are frequently more valuable if found used rather than in mint condition.

Specimen: When a new issue of a stamp is made available, a number of copies are stamped as "specimens" and are distributed to other governments or to internal agencies as samples of the new designs.

Surcharge: A surcharge is an overprint on a stamp that changes that stamp's value.

Tête-bêche: Two adjacent stamps that are upside down in relation to each other are described as *tête-bêche.*

Tied on: When a stamp is still on the original envelope, or a part of that envelope, and a cancellation carries over from the stamp to the paper, the stamp is said to be "tied

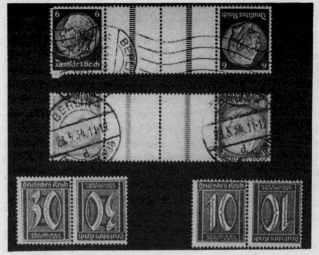

Examples of stamps that are *tête-bêche*, two of them with gutters.

on." Stamps still "tied" to the envelope are frequently desirable in helping to insure that both the cancellation and the stamp are valid and are not forgeries.

Variety: When a stamp is given a catalogue designation and number, the designation usually applies only to that stamp in a certain color and with a certain perforation. Occasionally, however, a stamp may be produced with a slight variation from the principal issue—for example, the color may vary or a different perforation may be used. These differences are known as varieties.

Vignettes: The principal part of the overall design of a stamp—typically a picture—is known as a vignette.

THE SCOTT CATALOGUES

While they are by no means the only stamp catalogues published, the *Scott Standard Postage Stamp Catalogues* are the ones you are most likely to need, at least when you are starting out as a collector. The catalogues have been mentioned earlier, in the discussion of the stamp albums published under the Scott name; these albums are keyed directly to the Scott catalogues. Chances are, you will want the catalogues for reference purposes, whether or not you buy the Scott stamp albums. Quite simply, despite their occasional shortcomings and frustrations, the Scott catalogues are the most comprehensive annually issued publications available, and are invaluable tools for any halfway serious collector.

The general catalogues come in four volumes. Volume One deals only with the United States, Canada, the United Nations, Great Britain, and the British Commonwealth. (There is also a specialized volume just for U.S. issues; this volume includes revenues and other nonpostal items as well.) Volumes Two through Four list the rest of the world in alphabetical order. If you are collecting the entire world, then you probably will want to get the entire set. On the other hand, if you are concentrating primarily on one country—Japan, for example—then you may need to purchase only one volume. Japan is catalogued in Volume Three.

What you get in the Scott catalogue is an essentially complete listing of every stamp ever issued for postal use in any given country. I say "essentially" because there is always argument over recognizing certain variations between stamps of the same issue, and it is one of the frustrations you are likely to encounter when using the Scott catalogues. For example, the confusion over color distinctions noted earlier in this chapter is further complicated by inconsistencies found in the catalogue listings. In some cases, color varieties among copies of an otherwise identical stamp are listed by Scott as different issues of stamps and each is given its own unique Scott number. In other instances, these color differences are noted as varieties of the same issue, and are given subnumber listings (instead of having its own number, the color variety may be listed for example as Scott Number 524a, with number 524 being the stamp in one color, and 524a being the same stamp in another color or shade). And then sometimes the color or shade variety isn't mentioned at all.

Despite these limitations and accompanying frustrations, you will still find the Scott catalogues an invaluable tool in putting together and enjoying your collection. Much of the terminology we have discussed earlier will be put into play in using the catalogues. There are, however, other technical considerations you will need to master in using the catalogues; fortunately, most are basic and easy to comprehend.

Let's look at some typical entries from a recent catalogue, in this case the 1991 edition of Scott, Volume One, which includes the countries that are or were a part of the British Commonwealth. The listings of the stamps from Barbados, an island in the West Indies, begin on page 285 of the catalogue and continue through 294. The entry begins with a brief geographical description of the island, followed by a sentence of historical information.

The Scott people have gone to great pains to provide helpful black and white pictures of all major varieties of stamps, and these varieties have in turn been given numbers indicating the design type. So in Barbados, stamp number 1 is pictured and given the design number of A1. All stamps using the same vignette will have the number A1. One unusual aspect of the first issues of Barbados is the fact that they carried no monetary notation, and the values were determined by the colors in which they were printed.

The first four stamps listed in Scott for Barbados are catalogued as follows:

1852–55 Unwmk. Engr. Imperf.
Blued Paper

1 A1	(1/2p) deep grn		100.00	200.00
a	(1/2p) yellow green		7,500.00	900.00
2 A1	(1p) dark blue		16.00	45.00
a	(1p) blue		16.00	45.00
3 A1	(2p) slate blue		10.00	
a	(2p) grayish slate		300.00	
b	Vert. half (#3a) used as 1p on cover			6,500.00
4 A1	(4p) brn red ('55)		30.00	110.00

No. 3 was not placed in use.
No. 3a was used only when bisected.

Okay, what we learn here is that these stamps were first issued in 1852, with the exception of No. 4 which was issued in 1855. There should be no watermarks in the paper on which these stamps are printed, and the paper should show a bluish color. The method of printing used was engraving. The stamps were sold in imperforated form only. All four of these earliest stamps are of design A1. Because the monetary designation is determined by color, it is important to be able to distinguish between these various colors.

You will note that stamp No. 2 is described as "dark blue," and that a variety of that stamp, No. 2a, is described as "blue." Stamp No. 3 is listed as "slate blue," while a variety—No. 3a—is given the designation of "grayish slate." (You should immediately see where some of the confusion can come from in distinguishing between these color variations.) Slate blue is rather distinct from blue or dark blue, so it shouldn't present a great problem. Distinguishing between blue and dark blue, however, can be more problematic, and you can readily see just how significant such a designation can become by looking at the value listing for stamps No. 1 and No. 1a. The value in the column on the left is for stamps in unused condition; the one on the right is for used copies. Stamp No. 1, a "deep green" issue, is valued at $100.00 in mint condition, while stamp No. 1a, described as "yellow green," is correspondingly valued at $7,500.00. There *is* a difference.

Likewise, there frequently is a significant difference between the value given used and unused copies of the same stamp. Stamp No. 4 is more than three times as valuable in used condition, and in such a situation it becomes apparent why it is important to leave the stamp "tied to" the envelope by a postmark, so that you can easily verify that the postmark is genuine and that the stamp is indeed a valid used copy.

As the note following these listings indicates, stamp No. 3 was never actually put into use, and No. 3a is known used only in copies cut in half and posted in its bisected form. Again, finding such a bisected copy still on its envelope is very important in validating its actual use.

A look at one other listing in Barbados will point out additional significant catalogue features with which you should have some familiarity:

1871 Wmk. 6 Rough Perf. 14 to 16

24	A1	(1/2p) yellow green	60.00	10.00
	a	Imperf. pair	625.00	
25	A1	(1p) blue	1,100.00	15.00
	a	Imperf. pair	1,300.00	
26	A1	(4p) dull red	750.00	37.50
27	A2	(6p) vermillion	500.00	35.00
28	A2	(1sh) black	190.00	15.00

The year of issuance for these stamps was 1871; they are found primarily in perforated form, although two of them (Nos. 24 and 25) are known to exist in imperforate form, unused condition only. All these stamps should have a watermark in their paper; in this case it is watermark No.

6 as designated by Scott. Every watermark ever used in the manufacture of paper for postal use has been given its own number designation for the purpose of the Scott catalogues. No. 6 happens to be a "large star," and a picture of it is given on the catalogue page where it is noted.

Stamp Nos. 27 and 28 are of design number A2. A sample of that design is also included on the page. And while it is not the case in this instance, were design A2 to be reinstated at some later date, after having been taken out of use for a period of time, the Scott catalogue would refer you to those later uses. This guideline is particularly important in instances where the same design has been used several times, but with variations such as different watermarks or perforation sizes, not always obvious and easily detectable.

One other aspect of the Scott catalogue system bears noting. All regular postal stamp issues are given a simple number. (Under Barbados, there are listings for 772 different stamps in the 1991 catalogue.) Semipostal stamps—of which there are only two listed in Barbados—are given a number with the prefix of B. Thus B1 for Barbados is a semipostal stamp issued in 1907. Airmail stamps (none have ever been issued for Barbados) are given a prefix of C. Postage due stamps are given a J prefix; official stamps are appropriately enough given an O prefix; special military stamps are listed with an MR prefix; and so on. Therefore, if you see a stamp listed as Hungary C5, it means that it is airmail stamp No. 5 as issued by Hungary. These prefixes are consistent throughout the Scott catalogues, and only seldom get complicated.

Another invaluable feature of the Scott catalogue is the extensive index in the back of each volume. Not only does it tell you in which volume you will find stamps from certain countries, it also serves on occasion to help you identify stamps that seem to have no recognizable country name on them.

As for the prices or valuations listed in the Scott catalogues, they are of major importance as a point of reference, but they are by no means absolute. We will deal with the issue again in our final chapter on stamps as an investment. Use these catalogue prices as guidelines in determining what you should pay for any given stamp, and use them in calculating the relative value of your own collection. But be aware that there is very little likelihood of ever realizing the catalogue value when selling stamps, and likewise when making a purchase you should always aim at paying less—sometimes considerably so—than the value listed.

5

Understanding the Basic Terms Used to Describe Stamps

—

The overall quality of a stamp collection is to a great extent determined by the individual quality of each stamp. You may notice that in many descriptions of stamps advertised for sale there are category designations for stamps by overall quality. "Fine" and "very fine" are the designations given most often, although they may be broken down further by such descriptions as "extra fine," "average," and so forth.

What these descriptive terms refer to is the overall quality of each stamp, taking into consideration many factors: Are all the stamp's perforations intact? Has the stamp ever been creased? Is the color true and bright, or has it faded somewhat? Is the stamp's picture well centered? Are the margins full? Is the gum on the back of the stamp—

assuming it is a mint copy, of course—even and undisturbed? Is there a thin spot on the stamp?

In the next chapter we will consider in some detail the various "tools" the collector needs in order to both handle and fully appreciate his or her collection. First, though, it is important to have a working knowledge of the basic technical aspects of grading the quality of stamps.

A glossary of key terms is a good starting point, and we'll begin with some of the descriptions of different conditions applied to stamps, designations that speak to the quality of the stamp in terms of collectibility and resale value:

As is: This is a term generally used in the sale of stamps with a *defect* of some sort. It means quite simply that you are forewarned that there is a *flaw* or *fault* in the stamp, and that once you buy it, it cannot be returned. Obviously defective stamps are to be avoided, but it is sometimes tempting to include them in your collection, especially when you may need only the one stamp to complete a set, or perhaps finish filling an album page. Or maybe it is a particularly valuable stamp when found in perfect condition, and you may rationalize that the only way you'll ever own it is to get a defective copy. I can't with any conscience advise you never to include defective or dubious copies of stamps—there are a number in my own collection—but do be aware that in terms of resale value, they are virtually worthless; just because you may have bought such a stamp doesn't mean that someone else will. Also, you should always be on the lookout for the best possible copy of every stamp, so hopefully you can eventually replace these "as is" stamps with perfect specimens.

Average: This term is something of a misnomer, because "average" is generally used to designate stamps considered to be of lower grade quality, stamps generally not of investment quality and certainly not of exhibition quality. The term—often abbreviated as AV or AVG or AVE—is used typically with regard to stamps for sale; average quality stamps generally sell for considerably less than better quality stamps. This "average" condition may be the result of any number of factors, including the positioning of the printed surface on the face of the stamp, the fading of the stamp's color, the clarity of the original impression, and the condition of the gum on the back of the stamp. Realistically, many stamps in any collection are of "average" condition, especially *used* stamps, and many older varieties of stamps are found almost exclusively in "average" condition.

Canceled: Stamps that have been used carry a mark to designate that fact and to ensure that they are not reused. These stamps are classified as "canceled" and the mark is a "cancellation." (See Used.)

Canceled to order: Stamps that have been canceled to order (designated commonly as CTOs), typically have been canceled in substantial quantity while still in sheets or panes and have not been postally used. Such stamps are typically issued by countries anxious to raise money by selling these stamps at a discount to collectors, and were never meant for actual postal use. The countries that have issued significant numbers of CTOs are those among the Eastern bloc nations—Czechoslovakia, Romania, et al.—and numerous "third world" nations, among them such "Sand Dune" emirates as Fujaira and Umm al Qaiwain, and Latin American nations such as Paraguay and Honduras. Among the larger nations, Russia has had a long-standing tradition of issuing CTOs. Many collectors are disdainful of these stamps, primarily because in most cases they were never intended for actual postal use. As I have stated repeatedly throughout this text, feel free to collect whatever you wish, and if CTOs are your meat, then fine.

Centering: Quite simply, centering refers to the position of the design on the face of the stamp, and how well the stamp is centered varies according to its position relative to the unprinted margin found between the design and the stamp's outer edges, typically the perforations. On perfectly centered stamps, the design is exactly in the middle of the stamp. Perfectly or well-centered stamps are the most desirable, and generally sell for a higher premium than those stamps which are off center, frequently denoted by the abbreviated designations CTT (centered to top), CTB (to bottom), and CTS (to side), which may itself be noted CTR (centered to right) or CTL (to left). Slightly off-center stamps are quite common and difficult to avoid.

Remainders and CTOs

Historically, some countries have made a practice of selling their stock of unused stamps when new issues are created to replace them. Many of these *remainders,* as they are commonly known, are canceled in some way—often with hole punches or overprinted with heavy bars—and then sold to philatelic merchants for resale to collectors. This practice was especially common among Latin American countries during the nineteenth century. While these remaindered copies of stamps are collectible, they are generally of less value and are less desirable than either mint or postally used copies.

Also less desirable are *CTOs*—cancelled-to-order stamps that are issued by many countries, most typically those in middle and eastern Europe. The practice of CTOs goes back to the latter part of the nineteenth century. In this instance, mint stamps are cancelled in sheets and are then sold to stamp dealers at a fraction of the cost of postally valid copies. Once the gum has been rinsed off these copies, it is difficult to distinguish them from postally used copies. Specialists usually can tell the difference, however, and should be consulted if you have questions concerning copies in your collection.

What should be avoided are stamps in which the design is
so badly centered that the stamp's perforations cut into the
printed surface.

Changeling: This term refers to the stamp's present color
versus its original color. Usually these changes in color
come about as a result of fading due to extended exposure
of the stamp to light. Sometimes, however, chemicals are
purposely used to try to create a color variety. True acci-
dental color varieties among various printings of the same
stamp are quite common, especially among older issues,
and some collectors make a specialty of these variations.
Chemically changed colors, however, are essentially a kind
of counterfeit—while the stamp, if mint, may still be of
value as postage, it will have little or no value to the collector.

Cleaned stamps: When a stamp is postally used, it is typically canceled with a hit of indelible ink which doesn't dis-
appear from the face of the stamp when it is soaked or
washed. Nonetheless, some unscrupulous persons may attempt to "clean" such a stamp, removing the ink cancellation (there apparently are fluids and/or chemicals that can
accomplish this feat). Sometimes such a cleaning is under-
taken so that the stamp can be reused for postal purposes.
More frequently, however, stamps are cleaned so that they
will be of greater value to the collector, since unused copies are typically of greater value than used ones. Frequently these cleaned stamps have also been regummed so
that they appear not only unused, but in mint condition. It
is a devious and insidious practice and, thankfully, not that
common. Easier to accomplish, however, and therefore
more common is the cleaning of a stamp to remove a pen
cancel. Such a cleaning can be particularly significant in
the case of some British Commonwealth stamps that were
made available for either postal or revenue fiscal uses. In
nearly all cases, these stamps have markedly less value if

fiscally used, and since many revenue cancels are pen cancels and therefore relatively easy to remove, one should approach unused copies of these stamps with a degree of caution.

Color shift: This term refers to the misalignment of colors on a multi-colored stamp. It is a fairly common production error, and is often no more and sometimes even less valuable than a perfectly printed copy. When a color is eliminated altogether, however, the result can be a very valuable error. Likewise, when one of the color printing plates is reversed or inverted, the mistake can mean big bucks for the lucky person who finds it. Recent turmoil in the Post Office has resulted in careless attention to quality control. The result has been an uncommon number of errors, one of which—a color inversion on the 1979 $1.00 candleholder stamp—got tremendous media attention. One thing to keep in mind, therefore, when looking through even the most common stamps in your collection is to be on the watch for errors. Chances of finding a true error, while still small, are increasing, and such a find can mean high value.

Condition: This is the general term noting the state of a stamp with regard to such characteristics as centering, color, hinge marks, and so forth. Many, many factors affect the condition, and it is the condition of the stamp which determines the stamp's relative value. The condition of a stamp may be given a range of designations, including but not limited to "superb" (abbreviated S or SUP), "extremely (or extra) fine" (XF or EF), "very fine" (VF), "fine" (F), "average" (AV, AVE, or AVG), and "poor" (P).

Crease: Any fold in a stamp which has resulted in a permanent mark is called a crease and is considered a major flaw, greatly reducing the stamp's value. Careful handling of stamps, utilizing the proper philatelic equipment, can help to minimalize the risk of creasing a stamp. Used stamps, however, are frequently creased through handling in the mails.

Defect: Any flaw in a stamp that has rendered it less than perfect and that reduces its monetary value. (See As is.)

Disturbed gum: When the gum on the back of a postally unused stamp has been damaged or altered in any way, it is said to be "disturbed." DG is the abbreviation you are likely to see, and it means that the stamp is considered relatively less valuable. (See Hinged and Never hinged.)

Error: Unlike a defect, which reduces the value of a stamp, an error may well increase the value. Among notable stamps classified as errors are the famous "Inverted Jenny," an early U.S. airmail issue in which the airplane (a biplane known as a Jenny) was printed upside down; a very few of these errors reached collector's hands, and today are very valuable. A more recent example of a highly collectible error was the color inversion on copies of the $1.00 Americana Rush Lamp Stamp, a denomination initially issued by the U.S. Post Office in 1979. The error was first detected in 1986 by a CIA employee in McLean, Virginia, who purchased a total of ninety-five of these stamps (apparently only one sheet of these stamps with the error—a total of one hundred copies—made it into circulation; five had been sold prior to the CIA employee's purchase, and have never surfaced). Current value for a copy of this error is approximately $15,000. Not all errors, of course, are so valuable, but it is certainly worthwhile to examine all stamps—errors are always possible, and they are part of what makes the hobby so much fun. Frequently, however, errors may not be so easy to classify. There are two related categories of variation—freaks and oddities—which, while collectible, are typically of significantly less value than true errors. When grouped with errors, the three classifications are usually referred to as EFOs. (See Freaks and oddities for a discussion of distinguishing characteristics.)

Extremely fine: Occasionally referred to as "extra fine" and typically abbreviated as XF or EF, this classification of *condition* denotes a stamp of high quality, just below the top classification of *superb.* A stamp graded "extremely fine" will have a design that is nearly perfectly centered, the perforations will be more or less even, the color will be bright, and the printing will be sharp.

Fakes: Frequently grouped with forgeries and counter-feits, fakes are every bit as insidious and sometimes harder to detect, especially for the beginning collector. Not to make it sound as if stamp collecting as a hobby is rife with crooks, but there does seem to be some overwhelming ten-dency on the part of some otherwise legitimate collectors to alter the condition of stamps. If a stamp has a fault— let's say a few perforations are missing—a clever (and devi-ous) person can carefully replace these little missing pieces to make the stamp appear whole. If a stamp is more valu-able in its used state, as opposed to mint, some collectors have gone so far as to attempt to recreate an authentic appearing cancellation and to cancel the stamp, then soak the gum off the back. Occasionally it may require an expert evaluation to determine if such a cancellation is or is not real. Usually less difficult to detect are efforts to remove a cancellation—often attempted when a stamp has been used for revenue purposes rather than postally—and to regum the back of the stamp. Fakes are a fact of life for philatelists, but if the collector remembers to check care-fully for repairs and washing, most can be detected and avoided. Many such fakes can be detected by the naked eye, either by holding the stamp up to the light or by soak-ing it in watermark fluid. In this way you may be able to see traces of an old cancellation that has been washed off, and usually you can make out the lines created when repairs have been made (new perforations added, for example). Other repairs may be less easy to spot—although some, such as regumming, you will learn to recognize in time—and when in doubt, it is best to consult an expert experienced in detecting fakes.

Fault: Any damage to a stamp which reduces its value and diminishes its collectibility is said to be a *fault.* A fault may be a *thin,* a missing perforation, a *crease,* a pinprick hole in the face of the stamp, a trimmed edge, a stain or ink smear (other than the cancellation), or even a tear. In other words, a fault may be barely noticeable, or it may be an obvious bit of damage—either way, it's a less desirable stamp than a completely sound copy, and collectors generally use them only as fillers. Occasionally, less common stamps are offered for sale or trade despite such imperfections, and should be duly noted (w/ flts).

Fine: A stamp deemed to be of "fine" (F) condition is, in fact, of minimal acceptability in terms of desirability to collectors. It's better than "very good," or "good," or even "average," but it's several cuts below the top rating of "superb." (I realize that these classifications of condition occasionally get a little picky—perhaps even ridiculous—but many dealers list their stamps in these various conditions and their prices vary accordingly, so it is best to be at least familiar with them.) A "fine" stamp is one on which the design is well off center, although not so far that the perforations cut into it. The color might not be as bright as desirable, and the actual printing may not be as sharp as on better quality stamps. Don't despair—the typical collection contains many "fine" stamps.

Flyspeck philately: This term generally is used to designate those stamps that are imperfect due to some minor difference caused by the printing surface itself (typically so small that it will appear as a flyspeck on the face of the stamp, hence the name). Because these imperfections usually are confined to individual stamps, these "flyspecks" are actually a form of "freak or oddity," as opposed to a genuine "error." You may also encounter the term *flyspeck philately* used to describe those stamps that can be distinguished from other similar stamps only by close and careful inspection under a magnifying glass. An example would be the minor variations found in the scrollwork borders of some early U.S. issues.

Forgery: Not a nice word under any circumstance, forgery is particularly bothersome to stamp collectors. The biggest problem is that there have been quite a few forgers busily at work almost from the first day of the first issue of stamps, and what makes it so confusing is that some of these forgers have been very, very good. Stamp forgery has also given rise to a whole area of literature devoted almost entirely to guiding the philatelist through the traps and pitfalls of forged stamps. As a beginning collector, you are not likely to be faced with many examples of forgery, mainly because less valuable stamps—the kinds you are most likely to be seeing initially—are not targets for forgers. Also, if you find a stamp on an old envelope, you can be fairly confident that both the stamp and its cancellation are real. It is primarily important for you to know that clever forgeries of many stamps do exist, and before you set about spending substantial sums of money on individual stamps, be sure you are doing business with a knowledgeable and trustworthy dealer. Remember also that deals "too good to be true," generally are. If you have stamps you feel need expert analysis, most dealers who are members of the American Stamp Dealers' Association (ASDA) are able and happy to give you an opinion. If you require the ultimate expert opinion you can contact either of the two recognized expert organizations: the Philatelic Foundation, 21 East 40th St., N.Y., N.Y. 10016, or the

American Philatelic Society Expertization Committee, Box
8000, State College, Pa. 16803.

    Somewhat distinct from forgeries, are counterfeits.
Whereas the former are aimed at duping the philatelist,
the latter are a form of stealing, generally from the government issuing the stamp. Forged and counterfeit stamps frequently look very similar, but usually forgeries are fake
copies made of highly valued philatelic items, whereas
counterfeits are illegal copies of current stamps, often of
the most common varieties. I'll use an example of a coin to
help you to better understand the distinction between the
two: if you create your own version of the common, everyday dime currently in use, you are a counterfeiter; if you
create a copy of an ancient Roman coin, then you are a
forger.

Freaks and oddities: Unlike errors, which are considered
highly collectible variations on a regularly issued stamp,
freaks and oddities constitute an area of the hobby that
many philatelists ignore. If you find a stamp on which the
perforations are out of sync with the stamp's design, so
that the holes appear in the center of the artwork, for
example, then you have found a freak. (It's virtually impossible to distinguish between freaks and oddities; both terms
are used, almost interchangeably, to describe imperfect examples of a stamp that are not true errors.) Other examples would include stamps on which a blob of ink has
smeared part of the design, or one in which a portion of
the paper was folded over during the printing process, resulting in a crease in the paper and a misapplication of ink.
Freaks and oddities generally are distinguished from errors
by the fact that they are varieties of stamps created by
chance and typically are not repeated consistently throughout an entire pane or roll of stamps.

Good: In terms of stamp condition, "good" (G) is not so
good. As a classification it falls somewhere between "fine"

and "average," and is not so frequently used as the other two are.

Hand stamped: Abbreviated as HS and H/S, and also known as hand canceled, this term refers to stamps or covers which have been canceled with the use of a hand stamp, as opposed to the routine machine cancel to which most stamps are subjected today. Hand cancels were used for many years, and some of the early postmasters created fancy cancels—star-shaped, diamond-shaped, leaf-shaped, circular whorls, and so forth—which are today considered highly collectible.

Heavily canceled: This term, abbreviated HC, denotes a stamp considered to be of lesser quality, and therefore of reduced value, due to an excessively heavy use of ink in the cancellation process.

Heavily hinged: (HH) (See Hinged.) A heavily hinged stamp has remnants of the hinge adhering to the stamp, enough so that it detracts from the quality of the stamp, and, therefore from its value.

Hinged: (Abbreviated H—what else?) When mounting stamps in a mint condition for display, many collectors use tiny bits of paper known as hinges to fasten the stamps in place. When the stamp is taken off its page in the album, and the hinge is removed, it invariably leaves a mark in the gum on the back of a stamp. The gum is now said to be "disturbed" and the stamp is classified as "hinged." If the gum shows only a trace of a mark where the hinge had been, it is said to be "lightly hinged"; if the gum is severely disturbed, or if pieces of the actual hinge still adhere to the stamp, it is said to be "heavily hinged." For many, many years, hinges were the predominant method used to mount stamps in albums, and as a result, it is relatively rare to find unhinged mint copies of older stamps (those issued prior

Examples of early U.S. stamps with "fancy" cancels. Some collectors
make a specialty of these.

to 1930 or so) which have been housed in collections. To-day, alternative methods of mounting stamps—principally plastic mounts—are available; they preserve the pristine gum on the back of the stamp and protect the stamps. As a result of this development, a battle has begun to simmer over the relative desirability of stamps which have been hinged. Indeed, the Scott catalogues typically make it very clear at some point in the chronological order of the stamps of each country that from a certain point on, all values are for never-hinged copies of stamps, and hinged copies are of lesser value. Some collectors have carried this search for the perfect never-hinged specimen of stamps to the extreme, making a near fetish of gum perfection, and treating hinged copies of stamps as virtual pariahs. I personally prefer to look at the face of the stamp rather than the back, and while I don't want to include damaged stamps in my collection, I really don't understand the whole fuss made over never-hinged copies. To each his own, however; a tendency toward anal retentiveness is a necessary part of every philatelist's makeup, I suspect, and never-hinged mania is probably just a further extension of the same trait.

Lightly canceled: When a stamp has been canceled in such a way that the greatest part of the face of the stamp remains clean, and only a trace of the cancellation shows, it is deemed to be "lightly canceled" (LC). Obviously, such copies are preferable to heavily canceled ones, and are generally of greater value.

Lightly hinged: (LH) (See Hinged.) A lightly hinged stamp has gum which shows only a trace of where the hinge had been. These copies are greatly preferable to heavily hinged examples.

Minor defects: This term, noted as MD, usually appears only in advertisements of stamps for sale. While many defects can indeed be "minor," they are still defects and should be avoided except in cases where you are desperate for a particular stamp. Also, be wary when ordering stamps noted as having minor defects—what is "minor" to the seller may be "major" to the buyer. (See As is.)

Mint: In ads for stamps, when you see the designation M, or the more frequently used symbol of an asterisk (*), it means that the stamp is in an unused condition. All the other abbreviations next to the asterisk provide more details regarding the condition of the mint stamp. "Mint" is one of four conditions noted for stamps which is absolute (the others are "used," "hinged," and "never-hinged"); most others are subjective opinions of the dealer who is offering the stamp for sale ("fine," "superb," "lightly hinged," etc.). With some rather notable exceptions, mint stamps are generally of greater value to collectors than are used copies.

Never hinged: (NH) Never hinged stamps are mint copies of stamps which have never been mounted in albums through use of adhesive hinges which stick to both the stamp and the album page at the same time. Collectors increasingly seem to insist on stamps which have never been hinged, and as a result such stamps typically carry a much higher price than hinged copies. (See Hinged for a more detailed discussion.)

No gum: Occasionally you will encounter stamps that show no sign of cancellation, but which also have no gum on the backs. These stamps are listed as NG (as a child, I assumed this designation meant "no good" and wondered why the stamp was being offered for sale at all), or occasionally as "unused," as opposed to "mint." These stamps generally have significantly less value than those with gum intact.

Off center: When a stamp's design is not centered evenly, but has greater margins to one or more sides, it is said to be "off center." Stamps whose condition is noted as "average" or "poor" are generally significantly off center; higher grade classification such as "fine" and "very fine" may have designs that are slightly off center. Generally speaking, the better centered a stamp's design, the greater the stamp's value to collectors.

Original gum: Noted as OG, this term is used primarily when referring to mint copies of older stamps. Occasionally you may encounter stamps on which the gum side has been regummed or doctored in some way to disguise either damage to the gum through hinging or deterioration through age. (See Fakes.)

Pen cancellation: Pen cancellations were generally used in the earliest days of postal operation—and for many years were common cancellations for fiscally used (revenue) stamps—and were replaced by either hand stamps or machine cancels. Typically postmasters drew a line across the stamp in ink or wrote his or her initials across the face (fiscally used stamps frequently show a date). Given the rather sloppy and careless procedures followed by the Post Office lately, pen cancels—and sometimes "Magic Marker" cancels—have become more common.

Perforated initials: Technically speaking, perforated initials (almost always called "perfins" and occasionally abbreviated PI) are not so much a designation of a stamp's condition, as they are a whole area of philately. I list the term here because perfins are quite common in older issues of stamps and can be very confusing to beginning collectors. Basically, these are stamps in which little pin-sized holes have been punched, often in the configuration of letters of the alphabet. This is done primarily as an anti-theft measure by businesses and by some stamp-issuing governmental departments. Some collectors make a specialty of perfins.

Precancels: Like *perfins,* precancels are not so much a "condition" as they are an area of philately. The term refers to a stamp that has been canceled prior to its having been actually placed on a piece of mail. Precancels are less common today than they were in the first half of the century, and while they are not peculiar to the stamps of the United States, they are particularly common on definitive issues of this country. Some collectors make a specialty of collecting precancels, perhaps focusing primarily or even exclusively on those from a particular city. Precancels should not be confused with canceled-to-order stamps.

Regummed: Sometimes noted as RG, regummed stamps have had a new layer of gum applied to the back of an unused stamp when the original gum has either been washed off or severely damaged. Regumming is not always easy to detect, and while it may make the stamp appear more attractive, it actually reduces its value, so beware especially of earlier issues which display a clear, even layer of gum. (See Fakes.)

Repair: A rather inocuous word for a rather insidious practice, stamps that have been "repaired" have in fact been worked on to disguise faults and damage which, if easily detected, would significantly reduce the stamp's value. (See also Fakes and Fault.)

Reperforation: "Reperforation" is a form of "repair" in which missing or damaged perforations have been carefully replaced, usually in order to make the stamp appear whole and therefore of more value. (See also Fakes and Fault.)

Reprint: When a stamp's original printing has been sold out and another printing is ordered, it is called, appropriately, a reprint. Frequently these reprintings occur some years after the stamp has gone out of use. What makes these reprints philatelically distinctive and important is the fact that the new stamp may be different from the original. For example, the original plate may have been somewhat blurred and the reprint may have an appearance different from the original. Or the original plate may have been altered in some way, or a different ink may have been used, or perhaps a different paper. Whatever the variance, for most reprints a distinction is made between them in the catalogues and they are frequently given different catalogue numbers.

Short perforation: When a stamp is described as having a short perforation, the truth is that one or more of the perforations is missing, or in philatelic vernacular has been "pulled." Because the goal of our hobby is perfection, a short perforation is considered a flaw of consequence, and the value of the damaged stamp is reduced accordingly.

Space filler: A space filler is any stamp in a collection that has a flaw and that should be replaced by a sound copy when one is available. Actually, availability isn't always the principal consideration—space fillers are typically damaged copies of more expensive stamps, stamps which when found in perfect condition are beyond the financial reach of most collectors. As a collector, I know whereof I speak when it comes to space fillers.

Superb: Stamps said to be in "superb" condition (usually noted as S or SUP) are of the highest quality, A number-1, top grade. What all this means is that the stamp's design is essentially perfectly centered, and there are no defects to the body of the stamp. You can expect to pay a premium for stamps listed as superb, but the more anally retentive of us would have it no other way. Be wary, however, of copies of the earliest issues listed as "superb"—in the strictest, technical sense of the word, such stamps are most uncommon.

Tagged: When a stamp is said to be tagged, it has been subjected to a process in which it is marked with an application of an invisible phosphorescent coating. This practice, called tagging, was developed to help speed the handling of mail through automatic sorting and canceling machines. This phosphorescent ink causes the stamp to glow when subjected to an ultraviolet light, so that special sensors on the postal equipment can locate and cancel the stamp. The special ink may be applied any number of ways, frequently appearing as a bar across the face of the stamp. As a collector, you will want to be able to distinguish these stamps—some even make tagged stamps an area of concentration—because they are frequently distinguished and given special places in specialized albums. The United States started tagging stamps in 1963. Other countries that frequently tag stamps are Great Britain, Canada, and France.

Tear: Plain and simple, a tear is a rip in a stamp. This is a major bit of damage and greatly reduces the value of the stamp.

Thin: Frequently noted as TH in descriptions of condition, a thin refers to a thinned area of the back of a stamp. Such damage may occur any number of ways, most typically when a hinge has been carelessly removed, or when a portion of the stamp's gum adheres to the surface of an album page. A thin reduces the value of a stamp, and because of this fact you should be especially careful of how you remove hinges and of how you put stamps in your album. Also, be on the lookout for repaired thins. (See Fakes.)

Unused: Technically, a stamp that is unused (UN) is one that has not been postally canceled, but that also no longer has its original gum. An unused stamp with its original gum is technically deemed mint. The two terms, however, are often carelessly interchanged.

Used: (U) A used stamp is one that has been canceled. It is usually noted either by the designation U or by the symbol ⊙.

Very fine: (VF) A stamp whose condition is listed as very fine is of high grade, relatively speaking. It is better than fine, but not so fine as extremely fine. In terms of condition, there should be no flaws, and the stamp's design should be no more than slightly off center. In terms of investment, very fine is the minimal condition which an investor should seek. As with all aspects of the subjective listing of stamp condition, very fine can be difficult to distinguish.

Very good: (VG) Better than good, but not so good as fine, a very good stamp may show some slight flaws and the design may be significantly off center, perhaps even cut by some of the perforations.

Very lightly hinged: (VLH) (See Hinged and Lightly hinged.) On a very lightly hinged stamp, there is very little trace of the hinge that has been removed from the back. The gum remains virtually undisturbed. We are splitting hairs here.

Hopefully you have taken the time to read straight through all these terms associated with condition in stamp collecting. If you have, you will quickly begin to get the picture of just how subjective and variable these appraisals of condition can be. It represents the one truly imprecise area of philately, a hobby which otherwise has exact definitions and rules and classifications that, while sometimes seemingly unnecessarily complicated, are all comprehensible and workable.

The bottom line with regard to stamp condition is, set your own standard for what you want or will allow in your collection, and try out a few dealers until you find one that you feel matches your own taste and your own standards for stamp condition—in other words, your idea of what constitutes a "very fine" copy of a stamp will be the same as that of the dealer. This step is especially important if you intend to collect for investment.

6

The Tools of the Collector

In Chapter 3 we talked about the different albums available to stamp collectors, as well as the various alternatives to actual printed albums. In Chapter 4 we dealt with stamp condition; in Chapter 5 with the technical terminology you will encounter most frequently.

In this chapter we will talk about care and maintenance of your collection, and will deal with the great variety of tools available to collectors, tools that are designed to assist you in careful handling of your stamps and in making accurate determinations.

SOAKING STAMPS

Before you begin soaking all those stamps off their envelopes, ask yourself one important question: "Would this stamp be of greater value if I left it on its envelope?" The answer, while perhaps not so easy to determine, may well be worth the effort, because in numerous instances there are unique collectible features to individual issues, involving the period of time in which the stamp was used, or perhaps the way it was used, or maybe even the city in which it was posted. Except for the space factor—stamps are a lot easier to store than are whole envelopes—there is little advantage to hastily soaking stamps; leaving them on the envelope will certainly not diminish their value, and may increase it.

Once you have decided to go ahead and soak, however, there are several guidelines you should follow. First of all, select a container for soaking that is relatively shallow and preferably large enough to hold all the stamps you want to soak while preventing them from clumping together. Most importantly, make sure the container is clean; dirt and, *especially,* grease or oil may damage your stamps.

Always use cold water or water that is at room temperature. Tap water is fine. The rule against using hot or warm water is important because some inks will dissolve or smear in warm or hot water and may cause discoloration of the stamps. In fact, some colored envelopes—such as those used for greeting cards, in particular the bright red ones—should be sorted out and soaked only with like colored paper. Even in cold water, some of these envelopes will "bleed," and there will be irreparable damage to your stamps. If you notice this happening, immediately rinse the stamp in clean cold water; you may be able to prevent discoloration. Also, it is always best to change the water with each batch of stamps you soak to prevent any of the elements that dissolve in the water—the glue, for example —from coloring your stamps.

You should try to remove the stamps from the water as soon as they lift free from the paper, but it is always best not to be too impatient. Do allow the stamp to lift free;

otherwise you run the risk of tearing a stamp that has not had all its glue dissolved.

Once you have taken the stamp out of the water, place it facedown on absorbent paper to dry. Paper towels are excellent for this purpose. White construction paper and plain poster board also work well as drying surfaces. Be careful of using newspapers, however, for while the newsprint paper is absorbent, you run the risk of allowing the ink from the type to transfer to the wet stamp.

It is important that you dry the stamp face down because otherwise there may be some glue remaining on the back of the stamp that will cause it to stick to the paper as it dries. Some people blot the backs of the stamps as they dry to help prevent curling. If you attempt this, again use absorbent paper, and beware of allowing the stamps to stick to the blotting surface.

Once the stamps are dry, you should store them carefully to get rid of curling and to avoid creasing or wrinkling.

You can purchase from philatelic supply dealers specially made stamp drying books that consist of blotter sheets. These books help prevent curling as the stamps dry. I don't recommend them, however, because I found that in cases where the glue was not completely soaked off the stamp, they tended to stick to the pages and I tore some when trying to remove them.

There also are products available that are used to separate stamps from paper without soaking. I have tried one of these—"Super Safe Stamp Lift Fluid" from Collectors Marketing Corporation—and found it to be relatively satisfactory. It is ideal for removing a stubborn hinge from a used stamp, but much less practical than plain old water soaking for removing paper from any volume of stamps. This stamp lift fluid is also excellent if you only need to moisten a small part of the stamp. You can apply it with a brush, and because it is thicker in substance than water, it can be controlled so that is doesn't soak the whole stamp.

It also acts almost instantly, so that you can separate the stamp from the paper in a matter of seconds. The major drawback to this product that I have found is that it tends to make the stamp stiff and especially likely to curl. Overall, it can be very useful in preparing stamps for your collection, but it is far from essential.

STORING STAMPS

In Chapter 3, we discussed the various ways you may display your stamps. But what of all those "extras," the duplicate stamps that invariably accumulate? They need to be stored in some practical, safe way, but they don't necessarily need to be stored in such a way that they can be viewed. With this consideration in mind, there are many options available to you.

There are boxes, of course—all sorts of boxes, such as shoe boxes, cigar boxes, those flat boxes that department stores use—and they are excellent for storage, up to a point. As with all things involved with stamps, it is primarily important that the box be clean. It also should be free of anything such as staples which might snag or tear the stamps. If you put loose stamps into a box, be sure to use some care, especially when sorting through them. When left loose like that, it is easy for stamps to get creased or for perforations to be bent and damaged.

Standard stationery envelopes are fine for storing stamps. They are especially good for flattening stamps that have become curled in the soaking/drying process. Even better are glassine envelopes, especially manufactured for use in stamp collecting. These glassine envelopes are available in many different sizes and have the virtue of allowing visibility of the stamp while at the same time protecting it.

We discussed stock sheets and stock books in Chapter 3. "Stock" as a term generally refers to extra stamps, and these sheets and books were developed especially for stor-

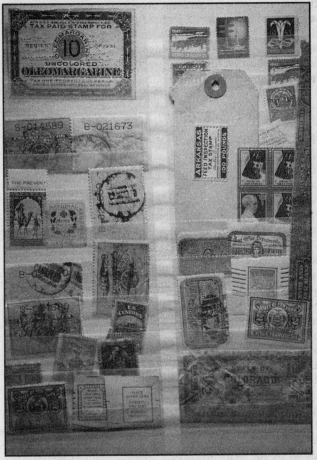

Revenue stamps and "Cinderellas" displayed on a stock sheet with glassine holders.

age of stamp accumulations. As noted earlier, these sheets
and books come in a number of styles and designs. The
best are the all-plastic sheets that allow full visibility of the
stamps. They are very expensive, however, and therefore
practical only for storing copies of some of your most valuable stamps. The other kinds of stock books and sheets are
all fine. Some are more durable than others, but they all
provide you with a safe and practical way to store your
duplicates. It is up to you, of course, to use care in employ-
ing any of these storage methods; you can damage stamps
in the very best stock book if you don't handle the stamps
properly and use basic common sense.

There are a few methods of storing that you should
avoid. When you get many copies of the same stamp, you
may be tempted to stack them together in a bundle and tie
them up much as you might newspapers. Don't do it, because the thread or string you use may well tear the
stamps, and some copies are bound to be bent.

Also don't just leave stamps lying around, especially if
they are exposed to strong light. Stamps will fade the same
as any printed item, and such "color changelings" are of
significantly less value than clean, clear copies. Stamps
should also be kept in a place that is dry and that never
gets too warm. Excessive heat can damage the stamps' paper and gum, making them brittle and causing them to
crack. Moisture may cause stamps to stick together, inks to
run, and will do irreparable harm. This is true whether the
stamps are loose, in envelopes, on stock sheets, or in albums.

Albums also need special care. They should always be
stored in an upright position. If they are stored flat, the
pressure on mint copies of stamps may cause the gum
eventually to adhere to the mounts or the pages. This kind
of pressure can also cause the ink to rub off some stamps,
or at least result in a transference of an imprint to the
surface pressed against it.

Careless treatment of your stamps can effectively di-

An example of a bad way to mount and display your stamps in an album.

minish the value, and, ultimately, the enjoyment of your collection. There is a story, apparently all too true, of a stamp collector who had one of the valuable "Inverted Jenny" stamps in his apartment. (The stamp, Scott No. C3a, has a catalogue value of $135,000.) When it disappeared one day, a search of the home turned up no trace of the stamp—until someone checked the bag in the vacuum cleaner. There was the (formerly) $135,000 stamp, bent, creased, and scarred, but still, fortunately, more or less intact.

Of course, few of us are likely to ever have a single stamp of such great value in our collections, but whatever stamps we do have are worth treating with care. And what if you do happen to acquire one or several stamps of significant value—what precautions should you take in protecting your investment against theft or damage or loss?

There are, of course, safety deposit boxes available at

most banks, and they do offer a relatively secure place to store stamps or even whole albums. Most of these vaults are temperature and moisture controlled, although you should be sure this is the case before signing up for one. The obvious disadvantage to safety deposit boxes is that you don't get to enjoy your stamps. Of course, there is a certain satisfaction in just *owning* them, but to really enjoy the hobby, you need to have easy access.

There are all sorts of safes you can buy for your home, and they may provide some security. If you do opt for a home safe, buy one that is labeled burglarproof but not one that claims to be fireproof. This latter variety comes complete with a system that saturates the safe's contents with a liquid in case of fire, not an ideal method of safeguarding stamps. It is also best to buy a safe that can be nailed down or in some way secured; otherwise you may have provided the burglar with a handy—albeit heavy—container for carting out your collection.

The best protection for stamp collections is proper in-home storage and stamp insurance. This kind of insurance is available from the American Philatelic Society, and information on such an insurance plan is available from the APS Insurance Plan Manager. The APS also will provide information on recommended home safes. In most cases, APS insurance offers full coverage against loss from theft from either bank vault or home safes.

TOOLS OF THE TRADE

Certainly the point has been well made by now that stamp collecting, in its most serious form at least, is not simply a matter of gathering stamps and sticking them on paper. There are many kinds of stamps and many factors to consider when seeking an accurate identification of any individual stamp. And for each of these factors—watermark, perforation, etc.—there is at least one tool the serious collector will need to help in determining just what stamps he or she has managed to collect. Likewise there are tools for use in handling and caring for stamps.

We will begin with the most basic of these philatelic instruments, and proceed through to the most esoteric.

Tongs: Tongs are one of the most important and basic tools a beginning stamp collector can have. They come in various sizes and shapes, and are generally inexpensive, costing typically anywhere between three and seven dollars. Because they really are a must for the collector it is important that tongs be one of your first ancillary purchases, and that you get to know how to use them right away. The reason for this is basic: you may not know it, but your hands carry acids and oils which can harm a stamp, especially through repeated contact. And thus, while it is obvious that you shouldn't handle your stamps while eating a hamburger, you also shouldn't handle them even though you have washed your hands thoroughly. To do so may cause irreparable harm.

Additionally, and more practically, just picking up a stamp is much easier with tongs. If you put a stamp on your desk or table and try to pick it up with your fingers, chances are you may crease the stamp or bend a perforation. As noted earlier, once a stamp is creased or loses a perforation, much of its value is diminished.

Most tongs are protected by being highly polished inside and out. This makes them easy to care for and to keep free of the potentially damaging oils and acids. Tongs should be kept dry and clean at all times, and it's not a bad idea to store them in the leather or plastic cases usually provided when you buy them. I keep a variety of tongs around with different tip styles. Since they are so inexpensive, it's not a bad idea to get a few different types and experiment with them. Once you get the hang of handling them (they may seem awkward at first, but you will quickly adapt), you will find them virtually indispensable.

Tongs are especially handy for putting stamps in mounts or for attaching them to hinges and putting them into stock books. These pointed little tools are much more effective than your fingers for getting into some of these tight spots without harming your stamps. I also find them useful when I'm soaking stamps to help remove paper from the back of a stamp. After you get used to them, you may find you're tempted to use your tongs for many functions around the house, but don't do it. Keep your stamp tongs for exclusive use with stamps. They are not tweezers, and they are not screwdrivers. To use your tongs for other purposes might damage the tips, which in turn might damage your stamps.

Watermark Fluid One principal way of identifying a stamp is by determining the type of paper on which the stamp is printed, and by detecting any watermarks which may appear in that paper. As we've noted repeatedly, one stamp may look the same as another to the naked eye, but a careful look at the paper and its watermark may determine that these stamps were produced at different times, and therefore are actually different issues. Virtually all stamp catalogues include pictures of the various watermarks you should be looking for, and will guide you in using them to determine any individual stamp's accurate catalogue number. First you should check the stamp by holding it up to the light, or by simply placing it against a dark surface; sometimes the watermark can be seen without the use of any aid. Assuming this tack doesn't work, then the preferred method of detecting a watermark and of distinguishing it from other similar watermarks is by putting the stamp face down in a small black tray and soaking it with a dose of watermark fluid.

There are several different trays available, but all serve the same purpose. Perhaps the slightly larger variety is most desirable because it will allow easier detection of watermarks in stamps that are in blocks. No version is very expensive, ranging in catalogue price from $1.00 to $3.00, approximately.

As for watermark fluid itself, again there are several varieties from which to choose, but all basically accomplish the same thing. I prefer Super Safe Philatelic Watermark Fluid—it has the virtue of being benzene free and therefore safe for watermarking even the delicate photogravure stamps that will fade in other liquids. A word of caution, however: read the label carefully; while there is no skull and crossbones on the package, there is a warning that "this fluid may be fatal, if swallowed." If a child is to be working with this fluid, he or she should be supervised, and if a very young child is in the household, then watermark fluid should be stored in a safe, secured place.

Watermark fluid, when out of the bottle, evaporates very quickly. It is best, therefore, to have the stamps prepared and in place before putting the fluid in the tray. Some watermarks will be immediately obvious, while others may have to be doused several times before you can make an accurate determination. Obviously, watermark fluid does not soften the glue on back of the stamp and does not cause sticking. In some cases, watermark fluid may even be helpful in removing adhesive tape that is stuck to stamps.

Another word of caution is in order: you may hear that watermark fluid is unnecessary, and that plain old lighter fluid (carbon tetrachloride) will do the job just as well. Indeed, lighter fluid will allow you to detect watermarks in stamps, but it also will set you and your stamps on fire if you aren't very careful. Watermark fluid is not flammable and should always be used in lieu of lighter fluid.

Another way to determine the watermark on a stamp is by using a Signoscope. (The complete name is Signoscope Optik-Electronic Watermark Detector; it catalogues, complete, for just under $300; a smaller, more portable version is available for less than half that amount). The signoscope is an electronic device that presses the stamp under a lens and with the use of variable light control makes it possible to see the watermark without the use of fluid. These various electronic devices are too expensive to be practical for most collectors. And while they are of use in some instances where the watermark can't be determined with just the fluid, the extra expense may well not be justified.

Perforation Gauges In Chapter 4, we discussed stamp perforations, what they are and why it is important that you pay attention to them. Repeating one part of that discussion, you must keep in mind that in most instances a variation in perforation between two otherwise identical stamps means that they are treated as two distinct and different issues, and are given different catalogue numbers.

To assist you in accurately determining the different perforations of stamps, you will need a perforation gauge. The gauge is used to measure the holes that have been punched between stamps, and in fact measures the number of perforation holes that fall in the space of twenty millimeters.

A perforation gauge is very simple to use. You place the perforated edge of the stamp on the surface of the gauge and then move it from one row to another until the stamp's perforated holes exactly match the dots on the gauge. Thus, if you maneuver your stamp up and down the numbered rows and find that the top edge aligns exactly with the dots of the line numbered 12, then there are 12 perforation holes within the length of twenty millimeters.

If the stamp is perforated 12 on all sides, it is said to be perf. 12. If, however, the top and bottom edges are perf. 12, and the sides measure perf. 11, then the stamp is said to be perf. 12 × 11. (The top and bottom perforations are always the same; the side perforations are always the same. When a measurement is given as above, with two perforations—12 × 11—the first number always refers to the perforation on the top edge of the stamp.)

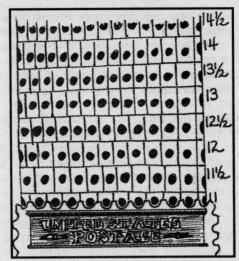

The perforations of a stamp aligned on a perforation gauge.

Gauges come in all shapes and sizes; they may be made of cardboard or of plastic or of metal. They may be square, or rectangular, or even round. They may cost as little as $.99 and as much as $37.50 (according to a recent philatelic supply catalogue). I happen to prefer using the first one I ever purchased—white cardboard with black dots and lettering—but that could be because it was the one I learned with, and it remains comfortable. All the gauges are fine, and if you are going to be doing a lot of intricate and complex calculations (it *can* happen) then perhaps the most expensive round variety with a detachable wheel to allow you to check the perforations of stamps still on covers is for you. You decide.

Stamp Hinges Stamp hinges have been used universally for years to affix stamps to an album page. They are very inexpensive, easy to use, and are eminently practical. Small packs of hinges can be purchased at all stamp shops or by mail; they are easy to store and tend to have a long "shelf life" if kept in a dry place. They are also a source of major controversy among collectors, and have, in fact, been the cause of much damage to stamps.

We have touched briefly on the controversy that has arisen over the insistence by many collectors that mint stamps be in a "never hinged" condition, since even the "safest" hinges tend to disturb the stamp's gum to some degree. I won't go into that discussion again here. Suffice it to say that while the insistence on gum purity can seem extreme at times, there is historically a basis of concern. In the earliest days of the hobby, and extending up into the first part of this century, many of the stamp hinges then manufactured caused damage, sometimes severe, to the stamps to which they were affixed. Today, however, we have what are termed "safe" hinges—ones that are completely and easily peelable from the back of the stamp. They are sold in packages of 1,000 hinges (catalogue price $1.20), and are available in a prefolded condition. Look for the words "peelable" or "removable" on the package.

Look at the hinge before you use it. It is made of a waxy, transparent paper; one side is gummed and the other is not. Note that the hinge is folded so that the gummed side is out; the fold should produce a short flap and a long one. Lightly moisten the short fold of the hinge and attach it near the top of the stamp and press down. Next moisten the long fold and mount the stamp on the album page. It's a very simple process and after a few trys you will be adept at it. Be sure not to lick too much, however, and be sure not to moisten the stamp as well, or it may well be permanently stuck to the album page. The idea of the hinge is that you can lift the stamp to see its back without removing it from the page. Or you can remove it to change it around or to replace it with a better copy of the same stamp. After removing a hinge, don't try to use it again. One use is all you can get per hinge. One word of caution: don't try to remove a peelable hinge until it has fully dried—it may tear the stamp and/or the album page.

Stamp Mounts Stamp mounts are the solution to the problems created by hinges and the only sure way to avoid the mark that hinges leave in the gum of mint stamps. Stamp mounts are clever devices in which the stamp is put into a kind of plastic pocket, allowing you to display the stamp without leaving any hinge mark. By putting the stamp inside the mount and affixing the mount to the album page, you have done nothing to detract from the value of the stamp. Furthermore, the thin polystyrene coating protects the stamp from dust and exposure. With mounts, stamps can easily be removed for inspection or to change them with another stamp of the same variety. Stamp mounts also make a much more handsome presentation of your collection.

Some of the mounts come with clear background and others come with a black background to allow the collector to more easily see the stamp's perforations. Mounts are manufactured by several different companies and come in an assortment of different sizes to accommodate the collector. A number of companies are now issuing stamp albums with pages that already include the appropriate sized mounts. These albums always make me slightly nervous, since some issues of the same stamp may vary slightly in size, and may not necessarily fit into the mount provided. These albums are also very expensive.

Stamp mounts are an expensive proposition any way you look at it, however, and in the long run the albums with mounts in place may be a bargain. Still I personally prefer to mount the stamps myself. Mounts are available either in precut packages or in long strips that you can cut into whatever lengths you need. I prefer the latter format, since there is very little uniformity among the stamp sizes of different countries.

Certainly you should use mounts for displaying any never-hinged mint stamps you have in your collection. Using mounts for all stamps, however, may prove prohibitively expensive, since the mounts generally cost anywhere from three cents to five cents each—and pennies turn into dollars very quickly when you are working with huge quantities of stamps.

The Guillotine If you decide to use stamp mounts extensively in your collection, you will find the guillotine to be an indispensable tool. Appropriately named, the guillotine is a small version of a paper cutter, and while it comes in several different sizes, the small ones will be used the most. Nonetheless, if you expect to collect mint blocks and souvenir sheets, you no doubt will want one of the larger versions as well. Much easier to use than scissors, the guillotine makes a nice clean cut and allows you to make repeated cuts of exactly the same size. Overall, its use will add a very professional look to your album pages. They also seem to last forever. I've cut thousands and thousands of mounts on the same guillotine, and there's never been a dull moment yet. And what do they cost? You can expect to pay anywhere between $10.00 and $35.00, depending on the size of the guillotine.

Magnifying Glasses Stamp collectors are definitely super sleuths. They have to be, because so much of the hobby involves detection. And just as Sherlock Holmes couldn't trace the identity of his villains without a magnifying glass, stamp collectors would be hard pressed to determine the identity of many stamps without the aid of a magnifying device of some sort. In fact, many early U.S. stamps were produced with such fine detail it's difficult even for experts to distinguish between them despite the use of a sophisticated magnifying glass. This distinction can be important. For instance, the value of early U.S. postage stamps can vary from about one to ten times depending on such minute factors as the detail of the ornament, frames, and designs—details that could never be seen without a magnifier.

The most standard glass used enlarges 16–20 times, allowing you to see most of the details on a stamp. Basically, the larger diameter glass will enable you to see most or all of the stamp at one time. The small magnifiers allow you to see part of a stamp in great detail, and can be especially helpful when you need to focus on one minute item on a stamp.

Two types of magnifying glasses used to look at the same stamp.

As mentioned, magnifiers come in all shapes, sizes, and strengths, as well as in many different configurations. The prices vary accordingly. Just keep in mind that the smaller the field of view, the higher the power; if you want to focus on minute details, then opt for a glass with a power of 20X. These magnifiers will not be cheap (generally in the $25.00 to $50.00 range), but you should never need more than one. You may, of course, also want a glass that will provide a broader view of the stamps, helpful when checking for overall quality. You can pay a lot for these as well, although it shouldn't be necessary. There are many manufacturers of magnification devices, so shop around and look for a good buy.

Color Guides Color guides are simply a smaller version of the color chips you'll find at the local paint store. By comparing the color on the guide you'll hopefully find it easier to determine the correct identity of the stamp. I use the terms "hopefully" and "easier" because most of the color descriptions given many earlier stamps are vague at best. For instance, I'm not thoroughly convinced that "olive black" is all that much different from "greenish black." These color differentiations go for just about every color of the rainbow and sometimes the people in Great Britain and the folks in the United States have different names for what I swear is the same color. Not to mention that the color of an old stamp may change or fade over the years, rendering the color guide not that helpful at all. At least, however, by having a guide you stand a chance at making an identification in some cases; without it, you would not have a clue. One bit of advice: if you specialize in the stamps from one particular country try to get a color guide produced in that country. There is no uniform color-guide for all countries. What are generally available are guides manufactured in Great Britain and Germany; both sell in the $15.00 range.

Drying Books Drying books were discussed briefly earlier in this chapter. They are used by collectors when soaking stamps. They are a helpful but not essential tool that provides the collector a place for the stamp to dry after being soaked while pressing it flat at the same time. Some people find these books more trouble than not. If you don't get all the glue off the back of the stamp, you run the risk of it sticking to a sheet of the drying book. Another problem I experienced arose when I left a large number of stamps in a drying book for several days; when I finally opened the book, I found that the stamps had mildewed. A rather obvious lesson, expensively learned. I prefer plain old paper towels myself, but if you want to try a drying book they are available in various sizes and with different numbers of pages. The prices vary accordingly, ranging from under $5.00 to more than $15.00.

Ultraviolet Lamp One of the more recent tools for the philatelist is the ultraviolet lamp, used exclusively to detect instances of "tagging" of stamps. Tagging was discussed in Chapter 5, and needs only a reminder here: It's a process whereby stamps are marked with an invisible phosphorescent coating in order to help speed the handling of the mail through automatic sorting and canceling equipment. It also serves to foil forgers.

Stamps that have been tagged will glow when placed under an ultraviolet or UV lamp. It is the only secure way to detect luminescence, and therefore has become an essential tool for any collector who wants to include tagged stamps as a unique part of his or her collection. (As noted earlier, the principal issuers of tagged stamps are the United States, Canada, Great Britain, and France.)

Ultraviolet lamps are available for as little as $13.95 (for longwave units that detect phosphorescence on stamps of Canada and France and several other countries) and $32.95 (for shortwave, used with stamps of the United States and Great Britain), to $350.00 and $140.00, respectively. It is not a tool that I use with any frequency, but it's one I'm glad to have.

Stamp Lift Fluid We discussed stamp lift fluid earlier in this chapter, as an addition to the discussion on soaking. Essentially, it is an alternative to soaking although not nearly so practical if a large volume of stamps is involved.

New developments are coming in this area of stamp care, so try to keep abreast of the latest items for sale.

Glassine Envelopes These specially manufactured envelopes are ideal for storing stamps. They are excellent for protecting stamps while still allowing maximum visibility, and they come in many different sizes, suitable to accommodate just about any sized philatelic item.

They are not cheap, however, and probably should be reserved for more valuable items. One hundred of the smallest sized envelope—2⅞″ by 1¾″—sell for $2.80 at current (1991) rates, while the same quantity of the largest size—11″ by 9½″—sells for $19.50.

Computer Software We've touched briefly on how computers are now being used by the post office to help speed the mail. Similarly, personal computers now enable collectors to find new ways to utilize systems in making their collecting easier, and information about their collection more accessible. Several different software programs are now available to collectors to assist them in many facets of collecting, ranging from organizing stock, evaluating its worth, to even creating special album pages. If you have a personal computer, chances are you'll be interested in looking into these programs, or perhaps even designing one that meets your own special needs. The major problem I find with these programs is the great amount of time it takes to input the vast amount of knowledge that can be programmed about each stamp.

If you keep your program simple, the computer can offer quick, specific recaps of reports, and these can be invaluable. For instance, if you want a report covering the value of your Iceland collection, input the catalogue number and value of each Icelandic stamp you own, and the computer can print out a complete list with the total value. This list could be used if you are interested in selling this part of your collection, or a printout could be put in your pocket the next time you go to a stamp show to aid you in looking for stamps that are missing from your collection. Updates of yearly values and additions to your collection are relatively easy to input. If you undertake such a program, instant reviews of your collection will be readily available, and rather than having to go to the album each time you want to check on a stamp, you can just take a quick look at your desktop computer.

In short, a computer stamp program can easily help you to prepare want lists, stock lists of duplicate stamps, and help you relate to trends in stamp prices. It's also not a bad way of keeping the value of your collection up to date for insurance purposes. The more input you provide your computer about your collection, the more information you can access instantly. It may not be as much fun as handling and looking through your albums, but a computer program certainly allows you easily portable information about your collection, and it is a lot more practical than carting catalogues and albums around with you.

Some Stamp Collecting "Don'ts"

In the course of collecting stamps, it is inevitable that you will make some mistakes in the way you handle your stamps, in the way you store your stamps, and in the way you purchase stamps. Even the most experienced philatelist is subject to human error and miscalculation. There are a number of basic mistakes frequently made by beginning collectors; the following are a few of the major "don'ts" to avoid:

- **Don't** handle stamps with your hands. There are oils in your skin that will transfer to the paper and may help accelerate fading of the stamp's color or the deterioration of the paper itself.
- **Don't** have food or drink near your stamps or your albums. It is so easy to make a mistake, and any slipup involving liquid can result in permanent damage to your collection.
- **Don't** leave your stamps lying about. Excess exposure to light and dust can cause them to fade and deteriorate. Stamp albums should be kept closed and stored upright on shelves. Loose stamps should be kept in stock books, in envelopes, or in boxes.

- **Don't** use hinges on mint stamps that have not previously been hinged. In today's stamp market, a premium is placed on copies of stamps that are in a "mint-never-hinged" condition, and while you may not feel so strongly about this point, you will find it a factor if you decide to sell or trade any of your stamps.
- **Don't** tear old hinges off the backs of stamps. If you simply yank an old hinge off a stamp, you may well either tear the stamp or create what is known as a "thin" in the paper, greatly reducing or even destroying the stamp's value. On used copies of stamps, soak stubborn hinges; on mint copies, let the remnant remain in place, and leave the removal to an expert.
- **Don't** automatically tear all stamps off their envelopes; many stamps are more valuable and more collectible if left on the original cover.
- **Don't** spend more money on stamps than you can afford. Think of philately as a hobby, and not as an investment. That way you are less likely to get burned financially.

STAMPS ARE US

No, there is no big supermarket-style store where you find mounds of philatelic supplies on sale at discount prices. For one thing, there just aren't enough of us. For another, we're not like that—most of us would rather take care of business from the comfort (and distance) of our own homes.

If you do want to venture out, there are stamp dealers in just about all major communities who sell philatelic supplies. And these same dealers usually can be found at any number of area and regional stamp shows or bourse, as they are also known.

Mail order, however, remains a major part of the stamp business. There are a number of large dealers who do extensive mailings to collectors all across the country. For reference purposes in putting together this text, I have used a catalogue from a major New York dealer, the Subway Stamp Shop. In addition to all the items we have discussed, there are many others available through Subway or any of the philatelic supply houses.

In order to locate these businesses that are always anxious to cater to your needs, you need only consult one of the number of periodicals available to philatelists. When I first resumed the hobby with full force a few years back, one of the great surprises I found was the whole world of literature devoted exclusively to the needs of stamp collectors. Not only are there books; there are also a number of newspapers and magazines.

And what I found most amazing is that four of these periodicals are published weekly. Weekly? What on earth can there be to say about stamps on a weekly basis? I asked myself. Then I subscribed and found out—it is amazing how interesting most of the content of these periodicals can be, and just how valuable a "tool" they have proved to be.

Now, I must confess I don't subscribe to all four. That to me would be overkill. I have, however, read each of them on occasion, and have settled on the largest among them—*Linn's Stamp News*—as my publication of choice.

Linn's, as it is known, has a circulation of approximately 75,000 on a weekly basis, and costs $33.00 a year to subscribers. It contains the news on the latest developments in all areas of philately, including the rather interesting developments in Eastern Europe that promise to yield whole new specialties for collectors to pursue. Articles abound on the new stamp issues from the U.S. Post Office, as well as on the mismanagement of the Post Office, and on the startling number of errors and screwups that keep surfacing as a result of this mismanagement.

Linn's also has columns that appear on a regular basis that are invaluable, or so I find them. There are columns that help solve confusing problems about individual stamps. Others keep readers abreast of the latest financial information on stamps—how things are selling, and at what prices. In addition, there are regular features on such points of interest as "Postal History," "Collecting on a Shoestring," "World of New Issues," and "Kitchen Table Philately." This latter column is a personal favorite that takes the reader through the joys and pitfalls of ordering bulk stamps for sorting and soaking.

Perhaps even more significant to some subscribers than the articles and columns are the many display ads throughout the paper offering stamps and philatelic supplies for sale, not to mention the dozen or more pages in each issue devoted to classifieds. Here you will find dealers who offer stamps and supplies for all ranges of collectors, from the rawest beginner to the most sophisticated specialist. It is in the classifieds as well that you can find collectors looking for trades, or for others who share some special area of interest.

Many of these same features and benefits are available as well to subscribers of any of the other three stamp weeklies, *Stamp Collector, Mekeel's Weekly Stamp News,* and *Stamps.* Each of these periodicals have the virtue of being somewhat less expensive than *Linn's* and also somewhat less daunting in terms of sheer size and volume. They also seem somewhat less formal, perhaps more "friendly" than *Linn's.*

One other point is worth noting. As in everything, you will find politics at work in the stamp world. *Linn's* has come under some criticism for the fact that it is part of the same company that publishes the Scott catalogues, and the news weekly has been accused on occasion of assuming an editorial position perhaps a little too squarely behind the Scott policies, some of which are—believe it or not—controversial.

You should look at all these publications and make your own decision on which to subscribe to, based on your own needs. If you are serious about the hobby, however, you will by all means want to subscribe to at least one of them.

In this age of constant change and new technical developments on an almost daily basis, virtually anything is possible. All the tools, all the latest gadgets described in the preceding pages may be outdated before you can read about them.

No matter, for while there really is a world of materials and information available to collectors, the only things that truly matter are the stamps and you, and the pleasure you get in enjoying the hobby any way you want. All the rest is window dressing.

A Brief Philatelic History

—

You know the old chicken-and-egg question about which came first, and so on. Well, it would seem fairly obvious that there couldn't have been stamp collectors around before the first stamp was issued, although I'm convinced that the two must have arrived on the scene at precisely the same time.

"Look! A postage stamp! I think I'll collect it," someone probably said, and so it has gone, on and on. Yet today, stamp collecting as such also includes a fascination with postal history, and in general with the ways we have communicated throughout the years.

You've probably seen some of those Cecil B. De Mille movie epics where messages are carved on stone tablets and then lugged great distances to be read by a king or a god or somebody equally important. Well, it apparently actually happened that way. One must assume that the sender was encouraged to keep the message short and to-the-point.

Then the Egyptians came up with a kind of paper made from papyrus (we're talking 2,400 B.C. here) and it got a lot easier to jot down your thoughts and send them off by courier. Certainly it was preferable to stone tablets, and as a way of getting messages around it lasted for many centuries.

Some ancient civilizations developed very sophisticated postal systems. Usually these were intended solely for use by the government. The Romans in particular had an effective method of transporting mails by both horseback and ship to reach the outer edges of the Roman empire.

Civilian usage of the postal system was allowed in both ancient China and in the areas controlled by the Aztec and Incan Indian tribes, although government mail was given preferential treatment.

The first postal routes established in England date back to 1533 and the reign of King Henry VIII. In North America, the British colonial government established a transatlantic mail link with England in the mid-1600s. Land transport of the mails between colonies came somewhat later. And while the sender—and/or the recipient—always paid a fee for the service, typically calculated on the basis of the distance the letter was to be carried, no one had yet come up with the idea of affixing a stamp to the missive to indicate that this fee had been prepaid.

It was an Englishman, Rowland Hill, a teacher and inventor, who first hit upon the idea of charging for the transport of mail according to the weight of the individual letter or parcel. He argued for the "penny post," the charging of a fee of one penny which would then enable a letter weighing no more than a half ounce to travel to any point in the kingdom. This fee would always be paid in advance, and to indicate this had been done, the so-called "Penny Black" stamp was created to be affixed to each letter. Hill was appointed head of the newly created postal service, and written communication entered a whole new era.

Great Britain issued this first actual postage stamp on May 6, 1840. Probably not coincidentally, the western world was at that moment poised on the edge of the great Industrial Revolution that so changed civilization, society, governments, people. Prior to that time the world had been a fairly small place, or perhaps it would be more accurate to say it was a large place made up of many smaller ones.

An individual's world used to consist of the town or community she or he grew up in. Within large cities, a person could live his whole life in a very small area, never venturing farther than a few blocks beyond his home. Friends and family lived there as well, so there was little need to communicate with the world beyond that small area.

That all changed when modern methods of manufacture and distribution replaced the more primitive systems of doing and making things by hand, for use by yourself or by others in your family or community. Suddenly there were many articles being mass produced, for shipment to other parts of the country, even to other parts of the world.

The first government to follow Great Britain's lead in issuing postage stamps was the canton of Zurich in Switzerland, in 1843. Brazil followed suit later that same year.

It wasn't until July 1, 1847, that the first nationally valid postage stamps were issued in the United States, although the U.S. Congress had established a postal authority and set postal rates some two years earlier.

The first efforts to organize a postal authority in continental North America had come much earlier than this date, however. Over one hundred years prior to the issuance of the first U.S. postage stamp, Benjamin Franklin had been appointed postmaster general for the American colonies, then still under British rule. In 1775, Franklin was named the first postmaster general under the aegis of the

Continental Congress (although technically the first postmaster general named after the establishment of the
United States under the terms of the Constitution was
Samuel Osgood, appointed in 1789 by George Washington).

Thus, when the first U.S. stamps were issued, one of

Important Events in U.S. Postal History

1847—The first adhesive postage stamp for use in the United States
goes on sale July 1st; use of these stamps will not be made obligatory
until January 1, 1856.

1860—The first Pony Express riders leave St. Joseph, Mo., April 3d
and deliver mail to Sacramento, Cal., ten days later, initiating a service
that will last little more than a year, but which will endure as a part of
American folklore. Pony Express proved to be a money-losing proposition and was effectively rendered obsolete by the completion in 1861
of the Western Union telegraph line between New York and San Fran-
cisco. At its height, the Pony Express kept eighty riders in the saddle at
all times of day and night, using Indian ponies in relays to cover the
ten or so miles between each of the approximately 190 stations.

1913—Parcel Post service is inaugurated January 1st by the U.S. Post
Office Department. Its initiation had been strenuously opposed by such
shipping outfits as Wells Fargo and American Express, but it proved to
be an immediate success.

1918—The first U.S. Postal airmail stamps are issued as regular service begins between New York and Washington, D.C. The first official
flight does not reach its destination, however, as the pilot gets lost and
lands in a cow pasture in Maryland. In ten years, the average airmail
letter will cross the United States in 31 hours, at a cost of 25 cents.

1920—The U.S. Congress enacts legislation enabling the Post Office
to accept first class mail not stamped with adhesive stamps, and the
Pitney Bowes Postage Meter Company is founded to produce an ac-
ceptable postage meter.

the persons honored was Ben Franklin. His likeness was featured on a five-cent issue (red-brown ink on bluish paper) and George Washington, the first U.S. President, was pictured on a ten-cent stamp (black ink, again on bluish paper). Prior to this time, many regional postmasters had created their own stamps (and established their own rates as well), some of which were ink hand stamps, and others actual pieces of printed paper.

Initially all mail was delivered to a post office, and a person was required to go there to pick it up. After the Civil War the system changed so that, in larger cities at least, letter carriers began the regular delivery of mail to businesses and private homes. "Rural free delivery" (RFD) of the mail was not initiated until the 1890s. Prior to that time, people who lived in the country—over half of the American population back then—had to go to the area post office to check on deliveries. Once rural free delivery was begun, and country folks were able to receive their mail at their homes, another major step was completed in bringing the various parts of the nation together. For these people, the rest of the world had become much more accessible and their own private worlds had gotten much larger.

THE UNIVERSAL POSTAL UNION

Meanwhile, the world's many nations were drawing ever closer together. In 1874, twenty-two countries attended a meeting in Bern, Switzerland, at which the Universal Postal Union was formed. Today the U.P.U. represents 169 different postal authorities, and since 1947 it has been a specialized agency of the United Nations.

Essentially what the U.P.U. has achieved is to connect all the various independent national postal services so that any piece of mail may be sent to any point in the world without undergoing additional charges at each nation's border. Thus a letter mailed from the United States to a small town in Australia will get there with only one fee paid—in the United States, where the letter originated—despite the fact that it will certainly be processed through two postal systems, and may have to pass through many hands before reaching its destination.

FDR, Presidential Philatelist

During the past century, there have been many noteworthy philatelists. Some of them were wealthy and were able to indulge their desire to own virtually any stamps they may have wanted. Others used more limited means to become expert in certain narrow areas, frequently contributing significantly to philatelic scholarship. Still others are remembered mainly because they were famous in ways having nothing to do with philately; they were simply famous people who collected stamps.

Certainly the most famous American philatelist of this century was Franklin D. Roosevelt. He began collecting when he was a child, and continued the hobby up until his death. In 1925 he was struck with polio, and it was at that time that he began to expand his collection significantly. Then when he became President of the United States, he saved the stamps from all over the world that came to the White House. He became so famous as a philatelist, that it inspired a whole new wave of interest in the hobby.

Perhaps the quality of his collection was not so outstanding as those of many lesser-known philatelists—he tended to be rather haphazard in what stamps he included and how he displayed them—but his contribution to the hobby was unquestionably great.

When Roosevelt died in 1945, his collection was put up for sale at a series of auctions. Because he had been so popular and influential, many people wanted to own some part of the official FDR stamp collection; as a result, the auctions were active and the money realized almost tripled the anticipated return. It is not uncommon today to see fragments of the FDR collection scattered among many individual collections.

Within this international postal territory, each country which is a member of the U.P.U. carries and delivers mail originating in other member states in the same manner it deals with its own domestic mail. This service is achieved through fees and standards which are set by agreement of U.P.U. members. These fees are uniform, and are increased only through agreement of the union members.

Each country has its own individual postal history, and is of interest to collectors of that particular country's stamps. Within the scope of this discussion, the focus will remain generally and briefly on U.S. postal history, although any thorough history would itself fill a hefty volume.

The careful study of postal history is a detailed, painstaking, remarkably rewarding pursuit, for it goes well beyond the mechanics of how postal systems are established and maintained, and how new developments have come about.

We have already mentioned two individuals who played significant roles in the development of the postal system as we know it, both domestically and internationally: Rowland Hill and Benjamin Franklin. In the annals of U.S. postal history alone there are dozens of interesting and important individuals worthy of note and study. Two Postmaster Generals are of special interest to stamp collectors: Will Hays (more famous as Hollywood's self-imposed censor) served as Postmaster General in 1921–22; during his brief tenure, he established postal provisions which were geared to assist collectors, most particularly the creation of the Philatelic Stamp Agency which today is a major division of the USPS. James A. Farley, who served in the office under President Franklin D. Roosevelt, during the years 1933–1940, also became involved in enlarging and enhancing the Post Office Department's philatelic services.

One of the most rewarding ways to study the development of the modern postal system is to observe how mail was transported. The early method of transport of letters was simply by foot or by horse or carriage between communities. Beyond local deliveries, seaborne mail services were established, following traditional trading routes. The first seaborne mail boats were called post barques and packet boats. Later a wide range of oceangoing sea vessels carried the mail to distant international ports. In cases where the sender was given the choice of a delivery by sea or by land, wind and weather became deciding factors. These first "postmen" had to possess a great deal of stamina in order to endure the elements, thus the famous motto, "Neither wind, nor rain, nor dark of night shall stay us in the completion of our appointed rounds." Their perseverance helped to realize the goal of open, easy commu-

James Farley—Postmaster

James A. Farley, U.S. Postmaster General during a portion of Franklin Roosevelt's term as President of the United States, was accused in 1935 of abusing his position when he ordered the production of some twenty different U.S. stamps in forms other than their original when issued to the public. Some of the special printings he had ordered were for stamps in imperforate forms; others were created in large printing sheets which resulted in stamps positioned in ways unlike those which had been sold publicly. Farley apparently had ordered these special printings so he could give these unique varieties as presents to influential friends and politicians, many of them stamp collectors themselves. Because of their legitimate issue and their rarity, these items were automatically of significant value to philatelists. When Congress learned of Farley's misuse of his position, he was ordered to reprint his special varieties and to make them available for purchase by the general public (Scott numbers 752 through 771), thus earning him a place of special recognition among philatelists.

nication which was to provide the lifeline of international development.

The development of the airplane led rather rapidly to the initiation of air postal service. The United States issued its first airmail stamps in 1918, and while initial postal airmail service was crude, these flights still afforded an improved method of delivering mail.

The introduction of airmail service offered philatelists a whole area of collecting, as new stamps were created, many of them depicting the planes used to transport the mails. Also, special souvenir mail postcards were issued for various routes and destinations, and first flights denoted on envelopes became instantly collectible.

Another aspect of postal history which is especially interesting and which constitutes a rich field of study for the devoted philatelist is the choice of subject matter on stamps: who has been honored and why (and who hasn't, and why *not*); the use of stamps for propaganda purposes; the events, both grand and arcane, which have merited their own commemorative stamps. Also of interest are the various methods by which stamps have been produced, and the attempts to make stamps both more attractive and less likely to either be forged or to be reused.

Alternatives to postage stamps have been around for a long time. As mentioned earlier, prior to the development of standardized postal service, there were the ink hand stamps developed and used by regional postal administrators. Also prior to the introduction of postage stamps, most letters were sent "collect," so that the person who received it was expected to pay the postage. This practice was allowed as an option until 1856, when the use of postage stamps to prepay postage on letters became mandatory.

To the present day, however, certain classes of individuals and organizations are allowed to send letters through the postal service without using actual stamps. Soldiers, for example, are permitted free mail services during times of conflict, a privilege first granted during the Civil War and most recently during the Persian Gulf War. Senators and congressmen are allowed free franking privileges (a "frank" in stamp collecting terms means simply sending mail without having to pay postage), and some collectors like to accumulate these facsimile signatures which are typically used in lieu of stamps.

Also collected by some philatelists are meter labels used instead of stamps. These tend to be extremely limiting, however, and I think I would find such a collection tedious in the extreme. No matter—to each his own. Postage meters are most commonly used by businesses; they are efficient and allow a regular, accurate tabulation of the postage charges incurred. Many post offices also regularly use postage meter labels, something you as a philatelist should avoid on your own mail.

In recent years, new technologies have resulted in new methods and means of communication. Just as the development of the modern postal service brought closer together people from all parts of the country and the world, so the development of such means of communicating as the telegraph, the telephone, radio, and television have made the world that much smaller.

Certainly all these methods of transmitting messages have offered alternatives to the mails, and the most recent development in the area of immediate communications, the FAX (or facsimile) machine, has seemingly overnight become as prevalent and indispensable as a mailbox. The FAX machine has revolutionized business communication, allowing offices in all parts of the world to transmit legal documents and to share written information in only a matter of minutes. As a result, many letters and other items are no longer sent through the mails.

It remains to be seen just what the Post Office will do to counter this defection among its customers. Until FAX machines are so widespread as to be in every home, surely the Post Office faces no serious threat to its operation. And then certainly there will always be junk mail.

Deciding What Subjects Are Depicted on Stamps

There is a rule, officially codified in the 1970s, that "no postal item will be issued sooner than ten years after [the honoree's] death." What this means is that before an individual may be honored by depiction on a U.S. postage stamp, he or she must be dead for a minimum of ten years. Sometimes this rule runs counter to public sentiment and the desire to honor some particular individual(s) who may have died, and for whom there is a demand for immediate recognition on a stamp. A case in point was the strong outpouring of sentiment in favor of issuing a special commemorative memorial stamp following the explosion of the Space Shuttle Challenger in 1986; the rule held and no stamp was issued at the time.

The reason for this ten-year rule is to allow the passage of time to provide for a more objective consideration as to whether a particular person, group of persons, or organization truly merits special recognition.

The decisions as to who or what is depicted on U.S. stamps rests with a fourteen-member group called the Citizens Stamp Advisory Committee. Some of the people on this committee are stamp collectors, but some also are not. The committee reportedly receives up to 30,000 letters a year suggesting subjects to be honored on stamps. Those selected are usually the most obvious candidates, although the committee occasionally must bow to political pressures and select less well-known personalities. Another factor in deciding what to select is the subject's relative popularity among stamp collectors. The U.S. Postal Service is anxious to print stamps that will be popular; as a result there are many stamps issued that depict such subjects as cats, media figures, and horses—not necessarily in that order.

If you have suggestions for subjects to be featured on future stamps, send a letter to the Citizens Advisory Committee, Room 5670, 475 L'Enfant Plaza S.W., Washington, D.C. 20260-6753.

8

A World with Borders:
Learning Through Stamps

When you first begin to collect stamps, you probably will perceive the hobby as essentially a matter of acquisition: hunt them out, identify them, put them in the appropriate spot. As you work with the stamps, however, and as you develop areas of special interest, you will begin to realize that something more is happening. For just as you learn *about* stamps, you learn *from* them as well—a remarkably painless and rewarding experience.

As a child, I collected stamps from all parts of the world. I didn't know it then, but I was becoming what is termed rather dismissively a "generalist." In philatelic circles, generalists are not highly regarded, and, in truth, specialists are more likely to actually contribute something to the hobby, at least in terms of adding something to the general body of knowledge.

Many specialists focus on a narrow area of postal history, looking for shreds of evidence to use in piecing together the intricacies of early postal service. An interesting example is found in the collecting of covers postmarked in the Virgin Islands during the 1850s and early 1860s, a period in which the ships of all nations moved freely among the many Caribbean islands. Most of these vessels stopped eventually at the port of Charlotte Amalie on the island of St. Thomas, an international "free" port, which meant that no tariffs were imposed on goods traded on or from the island. Because there were so many national governments then represented in the Caribbean—Great Britain, France, the Netherlands, Spain, Denmark—it was not uncommon to find British colonial stamps postmarked from St. Thomas, then a Danish possession, or to see the stamps of two or more islands affixed to the same envelope. As you can imagine, however, it is a very narrow area in which to collect, and the chances of making great new discoveries are limited. Nonetheless, the specialists persist, these archaeologists of philately, and in the process have amassed a rich history of the development of postal service in its first one hundred fifty years.

As a collector, if you plan to specialize, you will find a wealth of literature available on just about every subject or area imaginable. (These are frequently pamphlets; many of them are out of print, but available from one of the several regional stamp libraries—see the Appendix for locations.) Of course, if there is no literature extant on your own particular area of interest, then write something yourself. In the process, you will learn a great deal, and your effort will be a contribution to all philatelists.

But what about the generalist—is he or she really learning anything by grazing through piles of stamps, spending years in a kind of once-over-lightly exploration of the stamps of all nations? Well, as a generalist myself, I can attest to the fact that through stamp collecting I have absorbed a tremendous amount of information about the world, its people, and their societies. That I have done it "painlessly"—in fact, have had a great deal of fun in the process—makes a great argument for utilizing stamp collecting as an adjunct to the normal, more basic teaching/learning process.

A cause of great concern to many collectors today is the fear that young people no longer "connect" with the hobby. Obviously, this *is* a concern, and, if true, a legitimate cause for alarm, because the future of philately depends on attracting new recruits. Teaching children about stamps, therefore, becomes essential if the hobby is to prosper and continue, and using stamps as a tool of teaching presents an opportunity to introduce children to the hobby.

Learning about stamps is closely related to learning from them. Through the hobby one picks up bits of information on a variety of subjects. Every stamp has a story to tell, a history all its own, and can be used as the basis of a short lesson—a lesson also learned in a totally effortless way.

Some teachers have incorporated stamps into their class lessons, using them as adjuncts to regular programs. Stamps have the virtue of being familiar, friendly objects, and they serve to reinforce and "fix" facts that otherwise might not be grounded in the student's memory.

One of the major areas of learning that will be reinforced by working with stamps is geography. I remember as a child that the textbook lessons I received in the subject were greatly reinforced and given a strong basis in reality through my early exposure to stamps. As an adult, I have continued to learn about geography.

Look at a map of the world today—look quickly; it's changing rapidly—and compare it to one that shows national borders and configurations just prior to World War II. You will be struck by just how much things have changed.

Look, for example, at Africa. In the late 1930s, the

European powers such as Great Britain, France, and Belgium were in political control of almost the entire continent. Each of the colonies issued their own stamps, but they were in the language, and frequently the coinage, of their parent nation, and the designs reflected their status as colonies. Great Britain's King George VI was featured on the stamps of such colonies as Nigeria, Gold Coast, Northern Rhodesia, and Kenya/Uganda/Tanganyika. The French franc was the currency in use in colonial nations such as Dahomey and French Equatorial Africa. The Belgium Congo was an exotic outpost for an otherwise rather colorless European monarchy.

Look at a map of Africa today, and you won't find most of the countries or colonies mentioned above. The Belgian Congo is now Zaire; Dahomey has been rechristined the People's Republic of Benin, while French Equatorial Africa has been split into four different nations: Chad, Gabon, Congo, and Central African Republic. As for the British colonies, Nigeria still exists by name, but Kenya/Uganda/Tanganyika has become Kenya/Uganda/Tanzania, and Northern Rhodesia is now Zambia, while the Gold Coast is Ghana. And all these new nations issue stamps.

Farouk of Egypt: A Philatelic History

When King Farouk was born in 1920, Egypt was a country of minor importance, a nation buffeted by years of war and dispute. World War I had seen German and British forces warring over its possession; internally, events had not been much calmer.

Farouk's father, Ahmed Fuad, had assumed the Egyptian throne in 1917, an inheritance of a royal family whose years of reign had been tumultuous and unsettling for a country with such a rich history. Fuad was exceedingly proud of his son and had great hopes for him; the name Farouk, meaning "One Who Knows Right from Wrong," was especially chosen by Fuad. That the name proved to be prophetically

An example of an overprinted stamp. In this case, a stamp of the Belgian Congo has been overprinted to reflect the nation's new name.

inaccurate can be seen through the stamps issued in Egypt during Farouk's reign, from 1936 to 1952.

In 1928, Farouk's picture, that of a smiling young boy, appeared on a series of four commemorative stamps. His next philatelic appearance was not until 1937, a year after he assumed the throne, when a series of eleven definitive stamps were issued. A year later, special commemorative issues depicted Farouk and his bride, Queen Farida. In the ensuing years, Farouk's likeness continued to appear on regular issues of stamps, including one semipostal item, two military post stamps, and a series of airpost definitives. The slender, youthful form that graced the first stamps was replaced by an increasingly chubby face

A fairly typical souvenir sheet—this one is from Ghana.

and an ever-widening torso. What the stamps can only hint at is the dissipation that was occurring both physically and mentally within Farouk—scandalous tales of sexual excess and moral corruption swirled about him. A petulant, mischievous boy had turned into a tyrannical despot, amassing great wealth for himself while his people suffered.

Farouk decided to divorce Queen Farida in 1949, a move that further alienated him from his people, who had admired the queen. His second marriage in 1951 was commemorated by the issuance of a special stamp and souvenir sheet depicting the newlyweds. Finally, a year later, the people of Egypt had had enough of Farouk and his debauched lifestyle, not to mention his political bungling. The 1952 revolution brought an end to his reign, a fact that can be quickly deduced by looking at the stamps issued that year. The postal authorities reached all the way back into their archives to 1937 and began systematically reissuing earlier stamps depicting Farouk, but this time his face was obscured by the overprinting of three thick black bars. Not every stamp carrying his likeness was reissued in this manner, but enough so that the point was clearly made: King Farouk was no longer a part of Egyptian life, and if it were possible, they would eliminate him from Egyptian history as well.

The study of history is likewise the study of change. Recent history (the last 150 years, at least) is given visual reality through stamps. Germany serves as an especially rich source of study through which to view historical change, and its stamps have followed and reflected every phase of development and every step of history's movement.

The first stamps issued in what is today part of geographical Germany were those of Bavaria, then one of the German states; the year was 1849. The numerous other German states quickly followed suit: Baden in 1851; Bergedorf in 1861; Bremen in 1855; Brunswick in 1852; Hamburg in 1859; Hanover in 1850; Lübeck in 1859; Mecklenburg-Schwerin in 1856; Mecklenburg-Strelitz in 1864; Oldenburg in 1852; Prussia in 1850; Saxony in 1850; Schleswig-Holstein in 1850; Thurn und Taxis in 1852; and Württemberg in 1851.

Unless you are a stamp collector, or a student of German history, most of the above names probably don't sound familiar. In fact, most of these states had existed for many years as politically independent units within the loose realm of the German empire. Just as the need for national and international postal service was a by-product of rapid growth accompanied by radical social and political change in the first half of the nineteenth century, the combination of these loosely united German States into the empire of a unified Germany came as result of these same forces. The first purely "German" stamps were issued in 1872, although two of the original states continued to produce their own stamps for a period of time: Württemberg until 1900, and Bavaria until 1920.

A study of German stamps produced after World War I reveals a world of political and economic upheaval. During the 1920s, the country underwent a period of extremely rapid monetary inflation. Currencies—and the stamps based on them—became worthless. Printing presses cranked out crisp new mark bills and bright new stamps, often returning the stamps for an overprint increasing their value even before they could be put into general use.

So rapid was the change in currency value that many stamps of this period are exceedingly rare in a used condition. For example, the German stamp with the Scott catalogue number of 267 was issued in 1923; it is an overprint of 800,000 marks on a variety of 500 mark stamp issued earlier that year. That stamp in mint or unused condition carries a catalogue value of twelve cents; a certified used copy, on the other hand, is valued at $1,200—a ten thousand percent increase!

The German stamps of the 1930s reflect the kind of propaganda produced by the government of the Third Reich, and they herald the onset of events that led eventually to World War II. The stamps produced during the war likewise serve as documents of the time, many of them being brightly colored scenes of domestic tranquility that belied the terror of actual events.

Then, following the war, Germany was once again split into a number of different political entities, each of them having its own postal service. The Federal Republic (West Germany) was created in 1949, as was the German Democratic Republic (East Germany); each country issued its own stamps. Also issuing stamps for its own use was that portion of the city of Berlin occupied by the Allied forces;

for a brief time following the war, stamps were issued for other occupied areas as well.

This political and geographical makeup remained in effect until the remarkable events of 1990 and 1991 brought an end to a splintered and divided Germany. Just as the map is being redrawn and history books rewritten, so today are philatelists reshaping their own maps and records of events in Germany. It is a fascinating time for stamp collectors, in a particularly rich area of study.

Also exciting are the events that are taking place within the USSR. Many of the former Soviet republics had issued their own stamps prior to their absorption into the USSR, and philatelists are eagerly awaiting the reappearance of issues from those newly liberated countries.

German stamps, of course, are just one area of study one might undertake to combine an interest in history with the hobby of philately. For while the United States has not undergone such remarkable geographical reshaping, its postal history is also a reflection of the country's growth and the increasingly important role it has played in international politics.

Even more significant, however, is the nation's social history as viewed through U.S. stamps. As a nation, we have used postage stamps to honor our leaders and to remind people of important historical events. They have been utilized as well as a means of conveying political and cultural messages—in other words as propaganda. U.S. postage stamps have told us to register and vote, to save our soil and air, to support our youth, to prevent drug abuse, to save our forests, to drive safely, to love each other, and—of course—to collect stamps.

Postage stamps are marvelous documents of the times that created them. In reflecting our history, they have become a part of it. Philately presents a wonderful opportunity for people of all ages to learn about their individual countries and about the world as a whole.

To take full advantage of this opportunity to learn,

those of us who are stamp collectors have an obligation to attempt to involve others in our hobby. Stamp clubs are a great way to introduce people—especially young people—

Sand Dunes

Great Britain's political influence in the world extended deeply into the Middle East and lasted until the second half of this century. During the British administration of the area now known as the United Arab Emirates, very few stamps were issued denoting national origin. The postal affairs of such Persian Gulf states as Kuwait, Bahrain, Qatar, and Oman were administered through the post offices of India, with the stamps of India overprinted with the names of the individual states.

The situation changed slightly when India gained its independence in the 1940s. For a few years, postal administration was handled out of the city of Dubai, although no special stamps were issued during this period either. Instead, the stamps of the Persian Gulf Agencies of Muscat and Oman were overprinted with new values.

Then, in 1961, Great Britain surrendered administration of postal affairs for the area to the Gulf States. Special stamps were created for the Trucial States, but were used for only a limited time. By 1964, each of the states had begun to issue its own stamps, and they did so with a vengeance.

Soon, thousands of stamps—many of them spectacularly beautiful —were being issued bearing the names of the various "Sand Dune" nations. Unfortunately, there was virtually no demand for these stamps for actual postal use; instead they were sold through philatelic offices, for resale to collectors.

The seven tribal states that make up what is now known as the United Arab Emirates are Abu Dhabi, Dubai, Sharja, Ajman, Umm al Qaiwain, Ras al Khaimah, and Fujaira. Because of the "fantasy" aspect of the stamps issued under the names of these various states, many collectors refuse to include them in their collections. Others, however, make a specialty of these interesting and often remarkable stamps.

to philately, and to the experience of learning through stamps. Because the hobby can become expensive, it is important that youngsters initially be shown the simplest ways of assembling and putting together a collection.

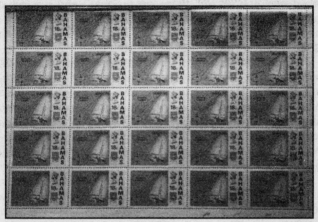

A pane of stamps from the Bahamas.

A potentially valuable adjunct to a beginner's stamp club is an organization called the Junior Philatelists of America, a nonprofit organization devoted to helping young stamp collectors learn about and enjoy the many aspects of the hobby. New membership is open to anyone age twenty-one or younger, and currently costs $9.00 a year. The JPA produces a magazine called *The Philatelic Observer* that goes to members six times a year. It provides a pen pal service to introduce young collectors to others with similar areas of interest; there is an auction department to assist members in buying and selling stamps; there is an exchange service to help members who want to trade stamps. In addition, there are a number of educational programs that members may use individually or as part of a club. For information on the JPA, write to JPA, Box 557, Boalsburg, Pennsylvania 16827-0557.

No matter what reasons may compel people to collect stamps, and no matter what goals they may have in mind when they first set out, there are residual—and somewhat subliminal—benefits that they invariably derive from the hobby. Stamps carry messages in and of themselves, and in these messages are worlds of information.

There is much more to be learned from stamps, however, than the bit of history each one reflects. To truly enjoy stamp collecting, I feel that you have to be part explorer, part mathematician, part historian, part scientist, and a great part skeptic. As you work with stamps, you learn to never take anything at face value, but to look beyond the obvious, to search for the unique thing that will differentiate one stamp from another.

In this respect, stamp collecting is a kind of science. Certainly some of the same techniques used in the laboratory are applicable in the handling of stamps. The inquisitiveness inherent in scientific study is an important component in the makeup of a philatelist. In my own case, this inquisitiveness perhaps was always a part of my nature, for while I never particularly liked either science or math as subjects in school, I always have chosen to work in areas where curiosity and constant questioning are important traits. I suspect that early enjoyment of stamp collecting as a hobby was at least in part responsible for pointing me in this direction.

I have enjoyed philately as a hobby for many years. In all that time, I have never stopped learning, and I know I never will.

9

Stamp Collecting: Hobby *versus* Investment

At the very beginning of this book, I asked you to consider why you are getting into the hobby of stamp collecting. I ask you that again: Why are you collecting stamps?

If you are collecting simply for the pleasure of it, then fine. There are tremendous joys to be had for the collector —the excitement of discovery; a sense of exploration and of adventure; the hours of concentrated fun in simply working with stamps.

If you are collecting because you find stamps beautiful, and you like to acquire beautiful things, then fine. Stamps, indeed, are beautiful, some of them exceptionally so. If you are a collector of topicals, you may be concentrating in areas that you find particularly attractive—flowers, for example, or perhaps depictions of great works of art.

If you are collecting because you want to learn, then

you are definitely to be commended. There is a whole history in stamps, both in the way they have been developed and in the people and events depicted on them. Learning from stamps, however, is not restricted to the knowledge you will gain about history—there is geography, there is politics, and there is the social record, a history of society and its people and culture as depicted on stamps.

If you are collecting stamps because you want to excel, because you want to gather an outstanding collection, one that is of exhibition quality, then more power to you. It is a difficult goal, one that takes intense devotion, absolute dedication, tremendous concentration, and—unless you are very fortunate—probably a lot of money.

If you have gotten into stamp collecting because you want to make money, however, then you may be in for a long, hard lesson. As an investment, stamps are at best a chancey proposition, and at worst, a way to go very broke, very quickly.

THE INVESTMENT

First of all, let's look at what goes into creating a truly fine and valuable collection. There's the money: as we've noted throughout this text, just about everything connected with the *serious* pursuit of philately is expensive. The albums are expensive, the mounts are expensive, and buying all the gadgets you need will cost a substantial sum as well.

So does this mean that if you don't have lots of cash to pour into collecting, then you're not *serious?* No, not at all. But just as there is a dramatic difference between the person who has prepared to appear in a community little theater production and one who has studied and fought and struggled and compromised to make it to a starring role on Broadway, there are differences between levels of stamp collecting as well.

And just because the little theater performer may never

qualify as a professional doesn't mean that he or she isn't "serious" and can't get great joy out of performing. Likewise, you can be serious about stamp collecting without spending great sums of money. But without putting money into it, there's little likelihood of your gathering a world-class, competition-level collection.

I would encourage you to indeed be "serious" about stamp collecting, but be rational as well. Don't spend money that you can't afford, assuming that if you really need to cash in the stamps you've bought that they can be sold quickly and automatically for the same amount you paid. It doesn't work that way.

THE TIME

One of the greatest expenditures you will make as a serious collector is time. You will put hours into sorting through stamps—most of them with very little "real" monetary value—as you look for specimens that you need and want. "Time" is the principal reason huge boxes of unsorted stamps and related philatelic material sell at such relatively low costs. The dealer who sells you such an accumulation has no doubt taken a cursory look through the mass of material, his experienced eye quick to spot likely treasures. Chances are, he will find nothing of remarkable value and will forego a more careful investigation. To sort through all these stamps, checking individual perforations and watermarks would take hours of his time. Sure, he might find a few items that are unusual, a few stamps that might carry higher price tags, but is it worth his time? Probably not. He'd rather let the collector do the work him/herself.

Much of my collection has been put together by buying these accumulations. It takes many hours to sort through the stock cards, the envelopes full of stamps, the pieces of old albums, organizing them in some way so that I can begin considering which items will fill empty spaces in my albums, and which are duplicates to be placed in stock books. If I calculated the many hours I have spent "working" at my collection, and if I placed a monetary value on those hours, assuming even the relatively low minimum hourly wage rate, I'd have racked up a huge fee. Dealers, of course, attempt to include the cost of their time in the prices they charge, and that is only fair. But what if you decide to sell your collection? If you believe you will be compensated for the hours you have put into sorting and organizing and identifying and mounting your stamps, you are in for a major disappointment.

No, as a collector you have to accept the fact that those hours represent an investment of time in the fun of collecting; the rewards are those of personal satisfaction and pride.

But wait, you say. What of those stories you read of people who find a rare item stuck among stacks of old envelopes, or even of rare postal mistakes that crop up periodically in brand new materials? Surely finding one of these extremely rare or unusual stamps will more than compensate you for all the time you've spent?

Of course it will. Several recent auctions of extremely rare items have resulted in record sales prices. An 1855 Swedish stamp, a three-skilling-banco issue, printed in yellow rather than the correct blue-green color, was sold for a then-record amount of $1.3 million. More recently, an early cover bearing the British Penny Black—the first postage stamp officially issued—sold for $2.4 million. (What makes this cover so special is the cancellation: the date of cancellation was May 2, 1851, the day after the stamp went on sale, and four days before it was actually valid for postage.) The same item sold at auction less than three years earlier for a mere $125,000.

These kinds of sales, however, are rare in the extreme, and the nineteen-times increase in valuation for the Penny Black cover is more than a little unusual. Of course, if you are lucky enough to stumble on something rare and heretofore undiscovered, then all your hours of searching and sorting will be greatly rewarded. But to undertake all the work in the belief that you will find such a rarity is foolhardy. You must do the work because you love the hobby; a surprise reward will simply further justify that love.

THE MONEY

And so what of the money you put into your collection: Is that money well spent? Is it a good investment? These are two distinct questions, and for the sake of coherence, let's look at the second question first.

Is money put into a stamp collection a good investment? Well, it all depends. It depends on whether you are looking to turn a fast buck—you know, buy low today, sell high tomorrow. If that's your goal, then forget it. You may, indeed, find someone willing to pay more for a stamp or for a collection than you paid out originally, but your chances are remote of finding that person quickly and without a search of some sort.

Dealers have a stable of customers whom they usually have been servicing for some time, and are always on the lookout for specific items they know one of their customers is anxious to find. These dealers, therefore, may be in a position to realize a relatively quick profit on their investment. As a collector, however, you are much less likely to have the same contacts, or to be able to locate the potential buyer of your stamps with the same ease and speed.

Bhutan—The Kingdom of Fanciful Philately

When serious philatelists hear the mention of Bhutan, they instantly roll their eyes. No one really takes the stamps of Bhutan seriously, they say. Those aren't really stamps: they're junk, silly, ridiculous junk.

Well, serious philatelists may well be correct, and one would be well advised not to invest too heavily in postal issues from Bhutan. It is inevitable, however, that over the course of collecting for several years, one is bound to amass a number of these stamps from Bhutan, and even though they may be worthless, they sure are fun.

To set the record straight, Bhutan really does exist. It is a kingdom of some 18,000 square miles, with around one million population, located in the East Asian Himalayas, between Tibet and West Bengal. It is ruled by a hereditary maharaja—affectionately known as "The Dragon-King"—and it has two capitals, one for the winter (Punakha) and one for the summer (Tashi-Cho-dzong).

Perhaps it was the very remoteness of this kingdom that inspired its leader to issue such remarkable stamps, and so many of them. There are stamps that look like holograms, others with a 3-D effect. Some are molded of embossed plastic, so that the person or objects depicted stand out in bumpy relief. Others are miniature versions of great works of art, printed on a canvaslike backing and complete with tiny brush strokes that you can feel. Still others seem to be printed on pieces of metal; not foil—real metal. My favorites, however, are the wonderful little records, round pieces of vinyl with holes punched in the middle and groves that, so I'm told, hold strange and amazing sounds, things like snippets of Bhutanese history (in English, of course), folk songs, and the Royal Bhutan Anthem.

Records? For use as stamps?! you might ask.

Ostensibly, yes, but a debate rages between the purists and the Bhutan fanciers as to whether any of these "stamps" have ever been actually postally used, or whether they actually ever could be so used. Other countries—"real" countries, not the so-called Sand Dune kingdoms—produce some fairly strange-looking stamps, and somehow they manage to get used. (Tonga and Sierra Leone are both good examples of countries that issue a variety of odd-shaped, odd-textured stamps; both are relatively busy nations that use these stamps for actually posting mail.)

Bhutan may never emerge as an area for serious philatelic consideration, but as a casual adjunct to your collection, these oddities can be a lot of fun. And if you can find the right record player, they can be entertaining as well.

A sampling of the rather unusual stamps produced by the country of Bhutan.

Therefore, it is never wise to spend more than you can afford on any philatelic item. If there is a chance you might need your cash for other purposes, then don't use it on stamps, because finding buyers takes a substantial amount of time. You can, of course, sell your stamps or your whole collection to a dealer. Most of them are prepared to buy—or at least broker—collections for resale, but they will purchase your stamps at only a fraction of their actual catalogue worth. If you are forced to sell all or any part of your collection on short notice, you face a very real possibility of realizing no more than you paid and perhaps even of receiving less than your original investment.

How then, do you find buyers for your collection, assuming you have time to do the dealing directly yourself, and don't have to sell to a dealer? You can always put your stamps up for auction by one of the many auction houses. These establishments conduct public auctions on more or less a regular basis—usually several times a year.

When auctioning any part of your collection, you physically surrender the material to the auction house. One of their expert appraisers should then give you a ballpark figure on what you might expect to realize from the sale. Typically, that amount will become the minimum sale price for the lot to be auctioned, and anyone who wants to purchase your stamps must be prepared to pay some amount above this minimum. The auction house, of course, takes a commission out of the monies you receive, but your chances of realizing a realistic value for your stamp collection is likely through auction.

If you cut out the middleman completely—the dealers and auction houses—and sell your collection or part thereof directly to another stamp collector, then you probably will realize the greatest return on your investment. Such sales can be effected through classified ads in periodicals like *Linn's Stamp News,* or through stamp clubs, or perhaps through stamp exchanges that exist in some larger cities.

Now as to the other question, the one asking if money put into stamps is "money well spent," if you have gotten pleasure out of your collection, and if you have enjoyed the time spent working with it, then I think you can say that your money was "well spent." Financial investment and profit should not be your goal as a collector. Instead, think of it as a way to have fun and hopefully not lose money in the process. If you end up seeing a financial return, then great—but don't count on it.

HOW TO VALUE YOUR STAMPS

We've discussed elsewhere some of the ins and outs of the Scott catalogues, how to use them and what the symbols mean and so forth. But what of the values themselves— what do they mean?

When I first started collecting seriously—started spending more than casual sums of money, I mean—I quickly learned to rely on the Scott catalogues as the source of all basic information, including the prices I should be paying. One thing I realized immediately was that a stamp's "catalogue value" had virtually nothing to do with the actual value. The rule-of-thumb I learned in placing a value on any stamp was that I should not pay more than one third the catalogue value when buying individual items or groups of stamps in a set. As for large lots or whole collections, my goal became to not pay more than one tenth the catalogue value. Usually these larger collections are given an approximate value by the dealer—call it an educated guess—and none of the individual parts have been carefully catalogued and priced.

In 1990, the Scott people announced, amid a great uproar of controversy, that they were changing the way they valued items in their catalogues. From this point on, they explained, the values they placed on stamps would reflect more closely the real value—that is, the price you logically should expect to pay in buying single items or sets. As a result, the value given some stamps was cut by 50 percent or more, while others were cut significantly less, or remained the same, or even increased. All of these changes have led to some confusion, and a new yardstick (such as my original one-third value calculation) has yet to be found, or at least has yet to receive universal application.

What these prices actually should reflect are the latest trends in stamp sales. In other words, the catalogue value should be the price paid for a stamp in the most recent transaction that included that stamp. If no sale has been recorded since the last valuation, then the catalogue price would remain the same. This way, it remains nothing more than a record of what the stamp has been worth, but at least it provides some sense of real value.

Despite all these caveats and reservations, the Scott catalogues are by far the best tools available in placing a value on U.S. stamps, and they are adequate and easily accessible in valuing stamps from just about all other countries.

It is imperative that you understand a few points about catalogue value, however. (1) A stamp valued at $5.00 is worth that amount only if there is someone out there willing to pay that amount. (2) Just because a stamp is relatively rare doesn't mean that it is necessarily more valuable than other more common items—if there is no market for a stamp, then it doesn't matter that few copies of it are available. (3) The minimum value given any stamp in the Scott catalogues is five cents (to be raised to fifteen cents in 1993 catalogues, or so it has been reported), but that doesn't mean you will be able to realize a dollar in return for twenty copies of the same low-value stamp. The five-cents is an artificial minimum placed on the most common stamps just to reflect the handling costs incurred by a dealer in filling any order for that stamp.

Remember all these points when trying to place a value on your collection and you will not be too disappointed when you actually are offered a purchase price. Also keep this disparity in mind when insuring your collection. Is it better to place a higher value on your stamps, or should you use the lower, more realistic figure? Your insurer and/ or a tax accountant probably will have different answers. I prefer to list everything at catalogue value and to worry about the reality of that value when and if the occasion arises.

THE FUTURE OF STAMP COLLECTING

In the first chapter, I referred to the fact that there are some twenty million stamp collectors in the United States alone. This figure is provided by the U.S. Postal Service, and includes all those people who save occasional stamps for individual reasons, many because "they're pretty." These people may be "stamp savers," but they don't really qualify as true stamp collectors.

The American Philatelic Society, the national stamp club for the United States, has more than 55,000 members. Many of these memberships, however, reflect multiple collectors. A more likely assessment of the number of stamp collectors currently active in the United States is somewhere between 250,000 and 300,000. This figure includes all those people who are actively enough involved in the hobby to attend stamp shows, belong to clubs, subscribe to and/or read some of the various philatelic periodicals, and buy stamps and philatelic supplies with some regularity.

A major concern among serious collectors, however, is how to attract new people to the hobby. Increasingly among young people it is not "cool" to be a stamp collector, and many who might have pursued the hobby in the past, instead today concentrate on video pursuits, or on something seen to be more "hip" than stamps.

Pragmatically, one of the reasons for this concern is alarm at the shrinking market for stamps and philatelic products. Stamps are worth only what other collectors are willing to pay for them, and a diminishing market inevitably will mean diminished prices and lower values.

A look back at stamp values over the last three or four decades shows that prices of most stamps—excluding, of course, the most common examples—have increased substantially. Much of this increase is a reflection of inflation —simply put, the prices of everything went up, including stamps. This trend was especially apparent in the late 1970s, when many stamp values showed huge increases. Much of this increase was not just a reflection of inflation, however. Those years were also a period of increased speculation in stamps, with investors looking to buy virtually anything that looked like a safe hedge against inflation. The results were stamp prices that went incredibly high, fueling even further speculation.

Then, in 1981, when the U.S. economy began to improve, the bottom fell out of the stamp market. Prices plummeted, and a lot of people got burned. Or rather, those who were buying these stamps for purposes of investment were burned. Those who bought stamps because they wanted them, because they valued them as part of a collection—well, they overpaid if they bought high-value stamps during this speculative period, but they at least had the stamps to display with pride as part of their collection. Yes, the stamps could have been purchased for less if the collectors had waited, but unless there were some compelling reasons to sell these stamps, eventually, through gradual inflation, their value no doubt will increase to some point near the original price paid.

THE BOTTOM LINE

If you are a stamp collector, someone who loves the hobby and gets great joy from working with your collection, then stamps are a good investment for you. But do not put more money into buying stamps and philatelic supplies than you can afford at any given time. There simply is no guarantee that you can get that same amount of money back, at least in a forced-sale situation.

If you are merely looking for a way to make money, don't try stamps. They take too much time, too much study. Instead, buy stocks and bonds, or invest in gold, or put your money in anything in which there is an active market.

If, however, you are a true stamp collector, and you want to make money with your hobby, then you must be patient. If you buy cautiously and conservatively, purchasing stamps in large lots, then investing a lot of your time in sorting and identifying the stamps, you can accumulate a collection that may have an actual value greater than the amount you paid.

It is also vital that you pay attention to trends. Until a year or so ago, there was virtually no interest in stamps from mainland China. Today, however, due no doubt to recent media attention focused on China, those stamps show a steady increase in value. As a result, if you were to have a substantial China collection that you don't have a lot of interest in, now would be the time to sell it.

It's really too early to tell what the outcome will be from all the turmoil in the USSR, but several of the former republics already have begun issuing their own stamps. A number of them—most notably Estonia, Latvia, and Lithuania—have an extensive philatelic history. The stamps issued by those countries prior to their absorption into the USSR probably will experience an increased demand in the near future, and their new issues—assuming they continue to produce national stamps and discontinue the use of those from Russia—should be watched for investment possibilities.

Stamps as an investment are far from the best way to see a quick return on your money. Buying stamps as a collector, using reason and caution, and keeping a careful eye on trends, however, can prove to be both satisfying and rewarding.

APPENDIX

Throughout the text, we have referred to different organizations you can write to for information, or to clubs you can join. The following are names and addresses of just a few of the many, many organizations that exist solely to service stamp collectors.

Of foremost interest is the American Philatelic Society. The APS, which functions as a kind of national stamp club, currently lists more than 55,000 members worldwide. It is a source of reference for collectors in all areas, and offers a range of helpful programs. Members receive a monthly magazine, *The American Philatelist;* they are eligible to purchase stamp insurance through the APS; and they may ask to participate in the club's program through which members sell stamps directly to other members via stamp circuit booklets. To get information on the APS, and to get an application form as well, write to:

APS
Box 8000
State College, Pennsylvania 16803

Remember to include a stamp at current first-class rate to cover return postage.

In recent years, the U.S. Postal Service has become more aggressive in its efforts to service the needs of stamp collectors. Philatelic windows, geared to offer collectors the latest stamps in any form they may require, have been implemented in many larger post offices. In addition, the USPS publishes a catalogue listing all U.S. stamps ever issued, complete with a value attached. This *Philatelic Catalogue* can be gotten free from many post offices, or by writing to:

United States Postal Service
Philatelic Sales Division
Box 449997
Kansas City, Missouri 64144-9997

In addition to the catalogue and the many current individual stamps, the USPS Philatelic Sales Division also has created a number of kits that should be of interest to beginning collectors, including many devoted entirely to selected topicals. They also sell complete-year kits of some back-issue stamps.

When responding to ads placed by stamp dealers, check to see if they are members of the American Stamp Dealers Association. This organization monitors its members and establishes standards of ethical conduct. For information on how best to work with stamp dealers, you can write to:

American Stamp Dealers Association
3 School Street
Glen Cove, New York 11542

The ASDA also has a program whereby, for an annual fee, they will supply you with information on all its members, as well as on upcoming stamp shows.

If you are interested in joining a stamp club in your area, you might write to the APS for assistance in finding the one nearest you. Another source of information on local clubs is *Linn's,* the publisher of *Linn's Stamp News.* The publisher maintains a listing of all local stamp clubs that have registered with it, and as a service to its readers will, at your request, forward your name and address to a club in your area. Write to:

Linn's Club Center
Box 29
Sidney, Ohio 45365

At the same address you may order, for a fee, a *Linn's* publication, the *Stamp Club Handbook,* that will assist you in organizing your own club.

If you are interested in first-day covers, write to the U.S. Postal Service for information:

USPS
Philatelic Sales Division
First Day Covers
Box 449992
Kansas City, Missouri 64144-9992

They will send you a letter outlining the steps you must take to receive first-day covers through the post office. If you want more specific information in the area, or if you want to learn about the history of first-day covers and about how to buy and sell them, then write to:

American First Day Cover Society
14359 Chadbourne
Houston, Texas 77079

In addition to the APS and the AFDCS noted above, there are any number of societies that service stamp collectors with interest in particular areas. Most of these societies issue regular publications for members, and they all charge annual dues, typically at a modest fee. Included among the more active societies are:

American Air Mail Society
70-C Fremont Street
Bloomfield, New Jersey 07003

American Revenue Association
701 South First Avenue 332
Arcadia, California 91006

American Topical Association
Box 630
Johnstown, Pennsylvania 15907

Errors, Freaks and Oddities Collectors Club
1903 Village Road West
Norwood, Massachusetts 02062

Machine Cancel Society
3407 N. 925E
Hope, Indiana 47246-9717

Post Mark Collectors Club
23381 Greenleaf Blvd.
Elkhart, Indiana 46514-4504

Precancel Stamp Society
Box 160
Walkersville, Maryland 21793

United Postal Stationery Society
Central Office
Box 48
Redlands, California 92373

In addition to the societies listed above, there are many, many others devoted to various areas of interest to stamp collectors. To get an up-to-date listing of all these specialized groups, you can consult a recent issue of *Linn's Stamp News* or any of the periodicals devoted to philatelic pursuits. The American Philatelic Society also should be able to supply you with a current listing of these organizations.

Above we gave the address of the Philatelic Sales Division of the U.S. Postal Service. Virtually every other nation that issues postage stamps has a similar division devoted to serving the needs of stamp collectors. Most are even able to provide you with the latest issues of stamps at face value. To order from these various postal services, generally you are required either to provide a cash deposit to cover your standing order or to have the cost of stamps and the handling expenses charged to a credit card. There are far too many of these services to list all of them. Among the most popular are:

Australia
Philatelic Bureau
GPO Box 9988
Melbourne, Victoria 3001
Australia

Austria
Oesterreichische Post
Briefmarkenversandstelle
A-10011 Vienna, Austria

Belgium
Regie des Postes
Service des Collectionneurs
100 Brussels, Belgium

Canada
Philatelic Service
National Philatelic Center
Canada Post Corporation
Antigonish, Nova Scotia B2G 2R8
Canada

Denmark
Postens Filateli
Raadhuspladsen 59
DK-1550 Copenhagen V,
Denmark

France
Service Philatelique
61-63 Rue de Douai
75436 Paris Cedex 09, France

Germany
Versandotelle fur Postwertzeichen
Postfach 2000
6000 Frankfurt 1, Germany

Great Britain
Philatelic Bureau
British Post Office
20 Brandon Street
Edinburgh EH3 5TT Scotland
Great Britain

Israel
Philatelic Service
Ministry of Communications
Tel Aviv-Yago 61080, Israel

Italy
Ufficio Principale Filatelico
Via Maria de Fiori, 103/A
00187 Rome, Italy

Japan
Philatelic Section
CPO Box 888
Tokyo 100-91, Japan

Luxembourg
Direction des Postes
Office des Timbres
L-2020 Luxembourg

Mexico
Department Filatelico
Edificio de Correos
2 Piso, Tacubal
06000 Mexico 1, D.F.

Monaco
Office des Emissions de Timbres-Posta
Principalite de Monaco

Netherlands
Philatelic Service
Post Office
P.O. Box 30051
9700-RN Groningen
The Netherlands

New Zealand
Philatelic Bureau
Post Office, Private Bag
Wanganui, New Zealand

Spain
Servicio Filatelico International
Direccion General de Correos
Madrid 14, Spain

Sweden
PFA Postens Frimarksavdelning
S-105 02 Stockholm, Sweden

Switzerland
Philatelic Service PTT
Zeughausgasse 19
CH-3030 Bern, Switzerland

Vatican City
Ufficio Filatelico
Governatorate, Vatican City

Additionally, a very popular area for collectors are the stamps from the United Nations. You can get an order form for individual stamps or you can enroll in their automatic new-issue program. For further information, write to:

United Nations Postal Administration
P.O. Box 5900
Grand Central Station
New York, New York 10017

Earlier we discussed some of the literature available to philatelists. In terms of general interest, the principal publications are *The American Philatelist,* available from the APS, and the following news weeklies:

Linn's Stamp News
P.O. Box 29
Sidney, Ohio 45365

Stamp Collector
P.O. Box 10
Albany, Oregon 97321

Stamps
85 Canisteo Street
Hornell, New York 14843

Mekeel's Weekly Stamp News
Box 5050 fd.
White Plains, New York 10602

You should write to these periodicals directly to get current subscription rates.

There are far too many books available that are of interest to stamp collectors to be able to give even a representative listing here. Some are directed to the beginning collector or to the generalist; most, however, are directed toward collectors with special interests. Some of the books are available at general book stores, while others must be purchased through philatelic supply houses, through stamp dealers, or by direct mail. Look for ads for these books in such publications as *Linn's Stamp News*.

In the course of researching this book, I consulted a great number of sources. Principal among them are *Linn's Stamp News,* cited above, and four other publications. They are:

Herst, Herman Jr. *Fun and Profit in Stamp Collecting.* Amos Press, Inc., 911 Vandemark Road, Sidney, Ohio 45365, 1988.

Krause, Barry. *Collecting Stamps for Pleasure & Profit.* Betterway Publications, Inc., Box 219, Crozet, Virginia 22932, 1988.

Rod, Steven J. *An Introduction to Stamp Collecting.* Amos Press, Inc., 911 Vandemark Road, Sidney, Ohio 45365, 1989.

Scott Standard Postage Stamp Catalogues. Scott Publishing Co., Sidney, Ohio, 1989.

There are eight philatelic libraries in the United States open to the general public. Not all are open every day, and before visiting one of them you might write or call ahead for hours of operation and other information. These libraries are:

American Philatelic Research Library
Box 8338
State College, Pennsylvania 16801

Cardinal Spellman Philatelic Museum
235 Wellesley Street
Weston, Massachusetts 02193

Collectors Club Library
22 E. 35th St.
New York, New York 10016

Collectors Club of Chicago Library
1029 North Dearborn Street
Chicago, Illinois 60610

National Philatelic Collection Library
c/o Smithsonian Institution
Washington, D.C. 20560

Sunnyvale Public Philatelic Library
665 West Olive Avenue
Sunnyvale, California 94086

Western Postal History Museum
920 North First Avenue
Tucson, Arizona 85719

Winesburgh Philatelic Library
University of Texas
Box 830643
Richardson, Texas 75083

INDEX